DECISIONS AT GETTYSBURG

BOOKS BY MATT SPRUILL

The U.S. Army War College Guide to the Battle of Chickamauga

Storming the Heights: A Guide to the Battle of Chattanooga

Echoes of Thunder: A Guide to the Seven Days Battles
with Matt Spruill IV

Winter Lightning: A Guide to the Battle of Stones River
with Lee Spruill

Summer Thunder: A Battlefield Guide to the Artillery at Gettysburg

*Decisions at Gettysburg: The Nineteen Critical Decisions That
Defined the Campaign*

DECISIONS AT GETTYSBURG

The Nineteen Critical Decisions That Defined the Campaign

Matt Spruill

The University of Tennessee Press / Knoxville

Library of Congress Cataloging-in-Publication Data

Spruill, Matt.
Decisions at Gettysburg: the nineteen critical decisions that defined the campaign / Matt Spruill. — 1st ed.
        p. cm.
Includes bibliographical references and index.

ISBN-13: 978-1-57233-745-9 (pbk.)
ISBN-10: 1-57233-745-1 (pbk.)

1. Gettysburg, Battle of, Gettysburg, Pa., 1863.
2. Command of troops—Case studies.
I. Title.

E475.53.S76 2011
973.7'349—dc22
2010030038

CONTENTS

ILLUSTRATIONS

Photographs

Maps

Diagrams

PREFACE

My close association with the Battle of Gettysburg and the National Military Park began in 1985, when I was a student at the U.S. Army War College at Carlisle, Pennsylvania, and I became a frequent visitor to the battlefield and studied the events in the first three days of July 1863 with great interest. Dr. Jay Luvaas and Colonel Harold Nelson (later a brigadier general) guided me in these studies. These two War College faculty members regularly conducted staff rides and on-the-battlefield discussions as we students plunged into an in-depth study of the battle and the campaign. Throughout my time at Carlisle, I regularly drove the short distance to Gettysburg to walk the ground and explore some aspect of the battle I had been studying. Many times I would vary the route so I could drive along the same routes Lee's forces followed in late June 1863 as they complied with his order to concentrate in the Gettysburg-Cashtown area.

After graduation my close proximity to Gettysburg came to a temporary end. However, I continued studying the campaign and battle and eventually began giving presentations to Civil War Round Tables and other groups. Three different assignments and six years later, I renewed my close proximity to the battlefield when I returned to the War College as a faculty member. Part of my teaching duties involved conducting staff rides for students, officers of active duty and reserve units, and ROTC cadets. While a member of the faculty, I passed the written and oral examinations and became a licensed battlefield guide. This gave me exposure to individuals with a vast knowledge of Gettysburg, which they were willing to share. I spent my summers giving tours and the rest of the year reading, studying, and giving talks to various groups.

I began to ask myself what had caused the campaign and battle to develop as it did. Were any actions or decisions so important that they influenced everything that followed? Over time I began to develop a list of these decisions. These were decisions of such magnitude that, had they not been made, the events at Gettysburg would have played out differently. This is not to say that George G. Meade would have been the vanquished and Robert E. Lee the victor, although it might have happened that way. That is beyond the scope of this book. I leave it to the reader to decide if the outcome would have been different. However, the sequence of events leading to the outcome would have been different, the orientation of the opposing forces may have been different, it could have been a two-day or four-day rather than a three-day battle, and it may have occurred away from Gettysburg rather than around the town.

The critical decisions were chosen based on my military background and extensive experience on the ground at Gettysburg, a close reading of the voluminous primary material, and the even more voluminous secondary sources. Perhaps other historians might choose different decisions, depending on their training and background, and might interpret critical events in different ways. However, I firmly believe the nineteen decisions enumerated in this book are the core decisions of the campaign and the battle.

The campaign and the Battle of Gettysburg did not happen as a result of random chance. Events unfolded as they did because of a series of decisions made by commanders at all levels on both sides. There were many decisions made before, during, and after the battle. However, out of all the decisions made, there were nineteen critical ones that had a major impact on shaping the campaign and the battle. My criterion for a critical decision is that, after the decision was made, it shaped not only the events immediately following it but also the conduct of the campaign or battle from that point on.

Some of these were major strategic and operational decisions, while others were tactical. Some of the tactical decisions were minor but had major impact. Had they not been made, the character of the battle and the decisions that followed would have been different. The difference would have been of such magnitude as to change the sequence and course of events of the Battle of Gettysburg.

This is not another history of the Battle of Gettysburg that covers all of the events, happenings, and decisions. My assumption is that the reader will already have a basic knowledge of the battle. My purpose is not to offer a brand-new interpretive history of Gettysburg, but to lay out some basic facts and to present a relatively clear outline of a very complex situation. Without neglecting important details, this account is designed to present the reader with a coherent and manageable blueprint of the Battle of Gettysburg—something that is often hard to get because of the welter of detail about the events.

I have attempted to refrain from writing about whether a particular decision was good or bad. What appear to be good decisions under the right conditions can produce bad results under adverse conditions. Likewise, what initially appear as bad decisions can eventually bring positive results. Instead I have concentrated on the consequences of each decision and pointed out how it affected the campaign or battle.

The decisions are grouped into four specific periods. These include the time before the battle, July 1, July 2, and finally July 3 and afterward. A chapter is devoted to the presentation and discussion of the critical decisions in each of these periods. Within the chapters, each decision has its own subsection, identified by a heading such as "The Army of Northern Virginia Goes North," "Reorganization of the Army of Northern Virginia," and so forth.

There is value in being in close proximity on the ground to where a decision was made or carried out. Being there provides you the opportunity to view the terrain and the tactical situation as the decision-maker did. This in itself provides valuable insights. In some cases this is not feasible if you are at Gettysburg and the decision was made in Richmond or somewhere else in Virginia. However, most of the critical decisions were made and carried out at or in close proximity to Gettysburg. I have therefore included an appendix with a battlefield driving tour that will place you on the ground either close to where the decision was made or where it was carried out. Included with the stops are excerpts from *The War of Rebellion: A Compilation of the Official Records of the Union and Confederate Armies*. The spellings of some words are different today from what were common in 1863: for example, *entrenchments* rather than *intrenchments*. I have left the spelling and grammar as they appear in the original documents.

Moreover, this brief guide has a specifically practical purpose: to help a reasonably well-informed reader get through the battle *on the ground*. This history is the servant to a slightly different purpose than the purpose of the more traditional history; the goal here is to help the reader gain an understanding of the battle from the ground up. The interpretive elements are specifically designed to support the parts of the book that are more like a traditional guidebook. In a way this approach provides a different perspective on research into both the primary and secondary sources related to

Gettysburg—indeed, I hope it will be seen as a foundation for an invitation to do further reading on Gettysburg.

* * *

I wish to acknowledge and thank the many who assisted and supported me during the writing of this book. Foremost is the director of the University of Tennessee Press, Scot Danforth, and his editing, production, and marketing team, who guided me through the editing and publishing process. Among them are Gene Adair, Thomas Wells, Stephanie Thompson, Tom Post, and Cheryl Carson. A thank you also goes to Bill Adams for his excellent copyediting of the manuscript. Kim Flynn at the Columbine Branch of the Jefferson County, Colorado, Library gave me much-needed research assistance by finding and acquiring numerous out-of-print books and documents.

Gettysburg Park Ranger D. Scot Hartwig and Licensed Battlefield Guides Louise Arnold-Friend and David Friend read the manuscript and provided many valuable suggestions. Friends and fellow Civil War historians Bob Moulder and Bob Huddleston also reviewed the manuscript and offered suggestions for improvement. My friends and fellow Civil War historians Mike Lang, Nick Kurtz, and Larry Peterson provided constant support and encouragement. Special thanks go to my friend Ian Duncanson, who reviewed the manuscript and pointed out a decision that should have been included—and now is. As always, my wife and best friend, Kathy, provided constant support and encouragement as this work developed from concept to book.

Matt Spruill
Littleton, Colorado

INTRODUCTION

In the last summer months of 1862, the Confederacy was riding the crest of a wave that had the potential of fulfilling the dream of independence. West of the Appalachian Mountains, General Braxton Bragg led his Army of the Mississippi north from Chattanooga through middle Tennessee into Kentucky. There he joined with Major General Kirby Smith's Army of Kentucky, which had captured the Kentucky capital, Frankfort, and installed a pro-Southern governor. Maintaining an army on the Ohio River would bring the South three major strategic advantages. First, Kentucky would become part of the Confederacy, if not through secession, then through occupation. This would provide access to additional food, livestock, and horses. Second, a Confederate Kentucky would be a strategic buffer on Tennessee's northern border and protect the critically important "Heartland." Third, Confederate forces on the Ohio River would interdict a vital major river transportation route between the eastern and western Union. However, before these advantages could be realized, Union and Confederate armies fought the Battle of Perryville on October 8, 1862. After Perryville, Bragg retreated from Kentucky, and by mid-December his and Smith's armies were now combined into the Army of Tennessee, which was located in defensive positions near Murfreesboro, Tennessee. In that month a Union army from Nashville maneuvered against Bragg. The clash of these two armies at Stones River from December 31, 1862, through January 2, 1863, forced Bragg back into middle Tennessee.[1]

In the far West a small army under the command of Brigadier General Henry H. Sibley marched from west Texas into New Mexico, then north toward Colorado. Repelled by a Union force at Glorieta Pass, near Santa Fe, in late March, Sibley retreated back to Texas. This ended the Confederacy's only serious attempt to expand its borders on the southwest frontier.[2]

In March 1862 Major General George McClellan used sea power to outflank the Confederate army in northern Virginia and landed on the Peninsula. Although conducting a slow advance, by June his army was on the outskirts of Richmond. General Robert E. Lee had been newly appointed to command the Confederate army around Richmond. This force, which Lee had renamed the Army of Northern Virginia, unleashed a turning movement against McClellan that drove him away from Richmond and eventually caused his army to depart the Peninsula. Lee followed this with a brilliant campaign of maneuver that transferred the center of conflict to northern Virginia. At the Second Battle of Bull Run (Manassas), he soundly defeated Union Major General John Pope's Army of Virginia. Capitalizing on his success, on September 4 his army crossed the Potomac River into Maryland. Once his line of communication to the Shenandoah Valley and Virginia was secured, Lee planned to advance into Pennsylvania by way of the Cumberland Valley. One of Lee's objectives was to influence the 1862 U.S. congressional elections in favor of politicians more sympathetic to the Confederacy and against the war. This was not to be. Thirteen days after beginning the invasion, Lee's army fought the Army of the Potomac near Antietam Creek in the bloodiest day in American history. Although the Battle of Antietam was a tactical draw, Lee ended his invasion; his army recrossed the Potomac River and returned to Virginia.[3]

The year 1862 was the only time the Confederacy conducted multiple invasions of Northern territory. The next year the strategic situation was different. Two of the South's main armies, both in the Western Theater, were on the strategic defense. Only in the East did the Confederate Army of Northern Virginia assume an offensive posture. On this army alone rode the hopes of a favorable political situation gained by a tactical victory on the battlefield.

The summer of 1863 was a pivotal period in the Civil War. In the western region, along the Mississippi River, Major General Ulysses Grant was victorious at Vicksburg. His success reopened the Mississippi River to uninterrupted traffic and cut off that part of the Confederacy west of the river. In Tennessee and northern Georgia, the Army of the Cumberland, commanded by Major General William S. Rosecrans, conducted a masterful campaign of maneuver. Rosecrans maneuvered General Braxton Bragg's Army of Tennessee out of middle Tennessee, captured the vital railroad hub at Chattanooga, and pursued his opponent into northern Georgia. When

Rosecrans allowed his army to become spread out in the mountainous terrain, Bragg turned and tactically defeated his pursuers along Chickamauga Creek. Rosecrans's army retreated into the fortifications at Chattanooga. Here it gathered strength, received a new commander, and was reinforced. In November the Army of the Cumberland with elements of the Army of the Tennessee and reinforcements from the Army of the Potomac broke Bragg's siege lines and drove the Confederates back into northern Georgia.[4]

In the East, General Robert E. Lee's Army of Northern Virginia began the summer by carrying the war into the North for a second time. His army moved north in high spirits and with the expectation of great things to come. Having gone north to fight a decisive battle, by mid-July the Army of Northern Virginia was back in Virginia with the Army of the Potomac having won its first major battle against them. Never again would Lee have the capability to conduct strategic offensive operations. He was forced to a strategic defense with limited tactical offensive and counteroffensive capability.

Conversely, when the Army of the Potomac began its march north after the invaders, it was an army filled with self-doubt and low morale. On its return to Virginia in late July, it was an army with a renewed confidence in itself. It and its new commander, Major General George G. Meade, had a sense of having just gained a major battlefield and campaign victory in a war that had already became a watershed in American history.

The two opposing armies in the East maneuvered from central Virginia, through Maryland, and into southern Pennsylvania. For three days they were locked in combat around the town of Gettysburg. When it was over, they had fought the largest battle ever seen on the North American continent and provided a pivotal point in America's great war with itself.

CHAPTER 1

BEFORE THE BATTLE

The Army of Northern Virginia Goes North

In 1863 General Robert E. Lee was faced with a major decision as to what would be his course of action for the campaign season. Essentially, he had four options. He could remain on the defense in Virginia, conduct tactical offensive operations against the Army of the Potomac in Virginia, send part of his army to the West to assist at Vicksburg or some other point, or take his army into Northern territory.

Remaining on the defense in Virginia might result in additional local victories for Lee with a high casualty rate for the Army of the Potomac, but it would surrender the initiative to the Army of the Potomac's commander. Conducting tactical offensive operations in Virginia would be one step above remaining on the defense. Lee might be able to gain the initiative and force the Union army to respond to his maneuvering in order to protect Washington, but, at the end of the campaign season, other than inflicting casualties on each other, that would have probably been the only gain. Sending part of his army to assist in the West would have had the effect of forcing Lee to assume the defense in Virginia. These options may have resulted in high Union casualties that could have had an effect on the Northern home front and given strength to the rising sentiment that the price for preserving the Union was becoming too expensive. Over time this sentiment might have produced a positive benefit for the Confederacy.

Lee realized that remaining on the defense would probably lead to defeat as the Union's superiority in manpower and manufacturing continued to be mobilized. As all three of these options gave the strategic initiative to the Union army in the East, Lee rejected them. The greatest disadvantage for all three options was that none had the potential to develop an immediate political situation that could lead to a negotiated peace.

In 1863 there was continued rising opposition to the war by some Northern politicians and segments of the population. One of the first manifestations of this had been the congressional election of 1862, when Lincoln's party lost seats to the Democrats. As the war progressed into 1863, the opposition continued to gain strength. Many factors accounted for this. In 1861 few could see the war continuing for as long as it did, and by 1863 there was no end in sight. The total Union and Confederate dead would eventually reach six hundred thousand, of which many had been killed, mortally wounded, or died of disease by 1863. In addition, the monetary cost of the war was increasing, an unpopular conscription act had gone into effect, and there was considerable disagreement over the Emancipation Proclamation. Lee concluded that to take advantage of this Northern war weariness and discontent, he must, as he had in 1862, again take his army into Northern territory in 1863.[1]

By late December 1862 or January 1863, Lee had been considering what he would do during the upcoming campaign season. He probably talked about his developing concepts with Lieutenant General Thomas J. "Stonewall" Jackson, and by early February 1863 he had formulated the framework of his campaign into the North. On or about February 23, 1863, instructions were issued to Jackson's mapmaker, Jedediah Hotchkiss, to make a map of the Shenandoah Valley and its extension in Maryland and Pennsylvania, the Cumberland Valley, all the way to Harrisburg.[2]

Lee expected to accomplish three objectives by taking his army into the North. First, such a move would place him in an area that had been barely touched by the war. In this fertile area he would not only be able to sustain his army, but he could gather and send supplies back to Virginia for future use. A secondary benefit would be to relieve, temporarily, the Virginia countryside and the inefficient supply system from having to sustain Lee's army. Second, if the Army of Northern Virginia moved north from the line of the Rappahannock River, then the Union army would be forced to follow. The Army of the Potomac would have to maneuver so as to keep itself between Lee and Washington, D.C., and at the same time attempt to force a battle to destroy Lee's army or to drive it from Northern soil. Such a move would give Lee the operational initiative and preempt any Union campaign plans in Virginia. Third, Lee was seeking to engage and defeat the Army of the Potomac on Northern territory. The political effects of this would have been far-reaching, as there were groups in the North wondering if the war had not gone on too long and if the price of saving the Union was not becoming too high.[3]

Basic to comprehending what Lee was attempting in the summer of 1863 is an understanding of strategic and operational concepts. The most fundamental of these concepts is that military action at the strategic level has no meaning unless it supports the political objective. The Confederacy's political objective was to end the war with the Confederacy intact and recognized as a separate country from the United States. For the South to accomplish this, the North would have to be forced to cease fighting and let the seceding states depart from the Union. Three things could make this happen: Lincoln's losing the election to a peace party candidate, changing the composition of the U.S. Congress, whose members would then demand an end to the war, and a dramatic rise of the peace party that could influence political policy. Any of these changes in combination with the others might bring about the desired results. The only way the Confederacy could help create any of these changes was by a significant victory on the battlefield. A victory of that magnitude would have to be one where a major Union army was soundly defeated on Northern soil. This would preferably be the Army of the Potomac, which among other things was charged with protecting Washington, D.C., and had not yet had a clear victory over the Confederate army in Virginia. It is obvious that Lee understood this concept in 1862, as he wrote about it in his letters to Davis. For operational security he did not write to Jefferson Davis about his campaign plan in 1863. But that does not mean he did not understand and apply this concept to his campaign plan.

In the summer of 1862, Lee had shifted the center of the war in Virginia from a close proximity to Richmond to northern Virginia. After his

General Robert E. Lee. Library of Congress.

victory at the Second Battle of Manassas, he realized that he had the opportunity to take the strategic initiative. He therefore planned to invade Northern territory. Lee's objectives for going north of the Potomac River were to subsist his army, maintain the initiative, cause the Army of the Potomac to leave Virginia, and influence the 1862 U.S. congressional elections to such an extent as to create a political advantage for the Confederacy. As Lee was not able to meet with Davis prior to crossing into Maryland, he had to communicate his concepts to him by letters. These letters provide a written record of his operational thinking.[4]

This was not the case in 1863. Lee, to maintain operational security, wrote very little to Davis about his objectives in again going north of the Potomac River. There was a meeting between Lee, Davis, and Secretary of War James A. Seddon on May 15, 1863. There are no known surviving notes from this meeting, but indirect evidence indicates Lee's general plan of campaign and objectives were discussed and approved.[5]

However, Lee did write to one person of his objectives to influence politics in the North by this campaign—his wife. In a letter to her on April 19, 1863, he wrote, "If successful this year, next fall there will be a great change in public opinion at the North. The Republicans will be destroyed & I think the friends of peace will become so strong as that the next administration will go in on that basis."[6]

In a letter to Secretary Seddon just prior to Lee's army commencing its move north, Lee explained his reasoning for not remaining on the defensive. He wrote, "As far as I can judge, there is nothing to be gained by this army remaining quietly on the defensive, which it must do unless it can be re-enforced. I am aware that there is difficulty and hazard in taking the aggressive with so large an army in its front, entrenched behind a river, where it cannot be advantageously attacked. Unless it can be drawn out in a position to be assailed, it will take its own time to prepare and strengthen itself to renew its advance upon Richmond, and force this army back within the entrenchments of that city. This may be the result in any event; still, I think it is worth a trial to prevent such a catastrophe."[7]

Two of Lee's objectives in the summer of 1863 were to subsist his army in the North and to disrupt the Union army's campaign plans in Virginia by drawing it north after him. If this was all that was accomplished, when Lee's army returned to Virginia, as it must after a period of time, the strategic situation would not be any better after the campaign season than before it. To have a major impact on the war, Lee's army had to defeat the main Union army in the East while on Northern soil. Such a victory in Pennsylvania in the summer of 1863 may have created a political situation leading to a negotiated peace.

The decision that Lee's forces would go north in 1863 set the basic framework for the war in the East that summer and affected the war in the West. Many of the following decisions flowed from this basic one.

Reorganization of the Army of Northern Virginia

Lee began 1863 with his army organized into two infantry corps—commanded by Lieutenant Generals James Longstreet and Thomas "Stonewall" Jackson—a division of cavalry commanded by Major General J. E. B. Stuart, and an artillery reserve commanded by Brigadier General William N.

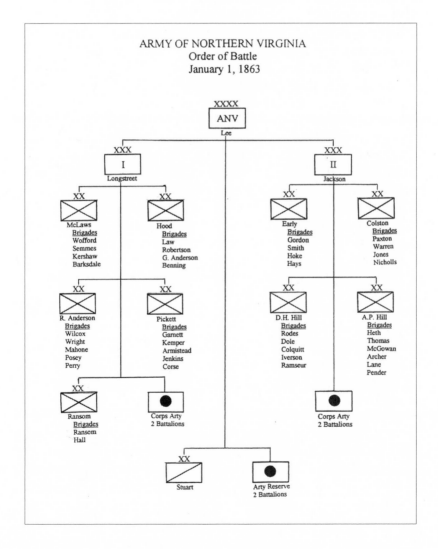

Pendleton. Each infantry division was assigned from three to seven artillery batteries. Each corps had one or two artillery battalions in reserve, while six batteries formed into two battalions constituted the army's artillery reserve. Lee believed that Longstreet's and Jackson's corps, with five divisions and four divisions, respectively, were too large, especially in wooded terrain, to be effectively maneuvered and fought. However, he had not taken the steps necessary to reorganize.[8]

After Jackson's death in May, Lee proceeded with a reorganization of his army. In a letter dated May 20, 1863, Lee proposed to Jefferson Davis that the Army of Northern Virginia be reorganized from two to three infantry corps. Davis approved Lee's recommendation, and on May 30, 1863, Special Order 146 reorganized the army. Lieutenant General James Longstreet retained command of his corps. Jackson's old corps lost A. P. Hill's Division and was reorganized with the three remaining divisions and placed under command of newly promoted Lieutenant General Richard S. Ewell. This resulted in two individuals, Robert E. Rodes and Edward Johnson, permanently being made division commanders. Reassigning Major General Richard H. Anderson's division from Longstreet's Corps and reorganizing A. P. Hill's old six-brigade division formed a third corps. Four brigades were formed into a division under Major General William D. Pender. The two remaining brigades and two other unattached brigades in the Carolinas formed a division commanded by Major General Henry Heth. Newly promoted Lieutenant General Ambrose P. Hill commanded this three-division corps.[9]

Lee's reorganization resulted in many of his key commanders being inexperienced in the positions of command they now occupied. There were forty-nine key commanders: three corps commanders, nine division commanders, and thirty-seven brigade commanders. Of these forty-nine commanders, fourteen of them, 29 percent, were new to the positions they now held. Two of these were corps commanders, and three were division commanders. This inexperience factor was critical at the corps command level. Being promoted from division commander to corps commander was a very large increase in responsibility and required the development of additional command and planning skills not needed at the division level. Although not quite so critical, the same also held true for the move from brigade to division command. In addition, the experienced commanders were not spread evenly across the army. In Longstreet's Corps the commander, the three division commanders, and all eleven brigade commanders, were experienced in the positions they held. In Ewell's Corps 35 percent of key commanders were inexperienced. They were the corps commander, one of three division commanders, and four of thirteen brigade commanders. Forty-seven percent of key commanders in A. P. Hill's Corps were inexperienced. They were the corps commander, two of three division commanders, and five of thirteen brigade commanders.[10]

Lee also reorganized the artillery. All the artillery batteries, except for the cavalry's, were redistributed to form fifteen battalions. With some exceptions, each battalion was organized with four batteries of four guns each, for a total of sixteen guns. Each infantry corps was assigned five artillery battalions that were under the tactical control of each corps commander and his corps' chief of artillery. This provided a corps commander the capability

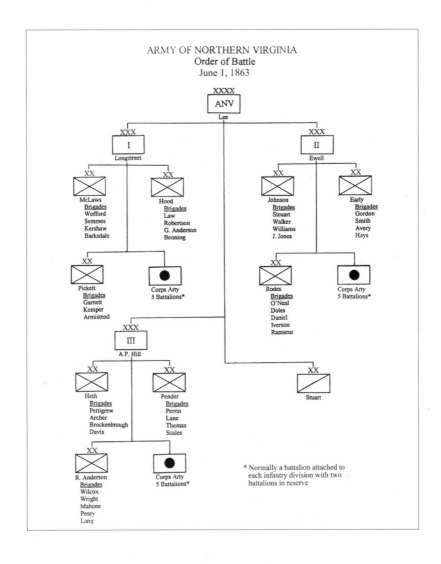

ARMY OF NORTHERN VIRGINIA
Order of Battle
June 1, 1863

* Normally a battalion attached to each infantry division with two battalions in reserve

to distribute or mass his artillery as individual situations required. Of the five battalions, each of the three infantry divisions usually had one artillery battalion attached for fire support, while the other two battalions were kept as a corps artillery reserve. However, this organization was flexible enough to keep more artillery in reserve or to attach more than one battalion to a division, if needed. In this reorganization all the battalions of the army artillery reserve were reassigned to the corps artillery and the army artillery reserve ceased to exist. While this arrangement provided more artillery to each corps commander, it left Lee with no army-level artillery he could directly employ to influence a battle. Having no central reserve of artillery or overall tactical artillery command, Pendleton confined himself to mostly administrative duties.[11]

The cavalry organization was basically left as it had been. However, to Stuart's normal complement of four cavalry brigades and six batteries of artillery were added two more brigades of cavalry.[12]

Lee's reorganization resulted in a more compact corps organization. In addition, it gave him more flexibility in maneuvering and deploying his army. Several times in the past, Lee, to carry out his plans, had been forced to take divisions away from their corps and place them under army control. This had resulted in fracturing command and control at the corps level and had also made Lee's span of control more complex as the number of commanders he had to communicate with was increased. However, while the reorganization alleviated those problems, it did have the disadvantage of establishing an unfamiliar chain of command in two of the corps.

The new structure had an influence on how the army approached Gettysburg, particularly with regard to how it was maneuvered and deployed for battle. While the reorganization streamlined and made the artillery more efficient at the corps level, Lee lost the capability to influence the battle with an army-level artillery reserve.

Reorganization of the Artillery of the Army of the Potomac

Any organization's capability depends on how it is organized. If different capabilities or missions are required, then the organization has to be temporarily or permanently reorganized. The Army of the Potomac began the war with a very decentralized and inefficient artillery organization. Four or more batteries were assigned to each infantry division, and there was no formal position for a division chief of artillery. Instead, the senior battery commander acted, without a staff, as the division's chief of artillery.

Nominally he had tactical control of the batteries, but in practice this was not necessarily so. The problem was further compounded when the batteries were attached to infantry brigades. Although this provided immediate fire support for the brigade commanders, it greatly hindered grouping batteries together at a decisive point on the battlefield. There were numerous instances of brigade commanders refusing to give up control of "their battery" when an attempt was made to concentrate the batteries of a division. As for concentrating artillery together at the corps level, this could not even be attempted. Only the army artillery reserve came close to an organization that could concentrate and deploy batteries at a decisive point.

The artillery reserve had been organized and placed under the command of Colonel Henry J. Hunt in September 1861. Hunt graduated from West Point in 1839 and was commissioned in the artillery. He had extensive service and experience with artillery, including service in the Mexican War. Just before the Civil War, he had been a member of a board that revised light artillery tactics. At the beginning of the war he was one of the army's premier artillery officers. Hunt, along with Colonel Charles S. Wainwright, who was the commander of the First Corps Artillery Brigade at Gettysburg, constantly advocated for reforms that would centralize the command and control and organizational structure of the artillery.[13]

The concept of centralized artillery had proven its worth at Malvern Hill on July 1, 1862. In this, the last of the Seven Days battles, all the artillery of Morell's division, which occupied the center part of the Union defensive line on Malvern Hill, was placed under control of the Second Brigade commander, Brigadier General Charles Griffin. Griffin, an experienced artillery officer, was able to position and effectively coordinate the fire of all of his division's artillery. Hunt's reserve artillery was positioned behind Morell's division. From that location Hunt effectively reinforced Griffin and also

Brigadier General Henry J. Hunt. Library of Congress.

13

supported other sectors of the Union defensive position. This centralization of artillery created havoc among the deployed Confederate artillery and attacking infantry.[14]

On September 5, 1862, Hunt was made the Army of the Potomac's chief of artillery and promoted to brigadier general. Malvern Hill notwithstanding, he was not able to convince his superiors of what artillery under centralized command and control could accomplish, and the organization was even more decentralized for the next eleven months.[15]

The Army of the Potomac's artillery organization took backward steps at Antietam, Fredericksburg, and Chancellorsville. At the Battle of Antietam, the artillery reserve was a small force of only seven batteries. It was increased to nine batteries at the time of the Battle of Fredericksburg. At Antietam and Fredericksburg, the artillery reserve was used to place long-range fire against Confederate positions. In both of these battles the reserve batteries were firing at and beyond maximum effective range and had less of a target effect than had the reserve been larger and better organized. A larger reserve with batteries grouped into brigades (battalions) and under a central command and control could have deployed part of the batteries closer to the Confederate positions while the remainder provided supporting fire.[16]

By the time of the Battle of Chancellorsville, the reserve had increased in size to twelve batteries. This reserve, with no intermediate command organization such as brigades or battalions, proved too large a span of control for its commander to command effectively.[17]

After the disastrous use of artillery at Chancellorsville, Hunt was able to convince the army commander, Major General Joseph Hooker, that a major reorganization of the artillery was required. He then implemented a series of changes that led to a highly centralized, responsive, and flexible artillery organization.[18]

On May 12, 1863, Army of the Potomac Special Order 129 organized all the artillery batteries into fourteen artillery brigades. Each brigade was under the command of an artillery officer, assisted by a staff. The artillery brigade commander reported directly to and was responsive to his corps commander. The seven infantry corps were each assigned an artillery brigade, the cavalry corps received two artillery brigades, and the remaining five brigades were grouped together into an army-level artillery reserve. Brigadier General Robert O. Tyler, who reported directly to Hunt, commanded the reserve. The reserve brigades could be temporarily assigned to an infantry corps or deployed independently wherever they where needed.[19]

The brigade strengths varied. Of the seven brigades assigned to the infantry corps, one had four batteries, five had five batteries, and one had

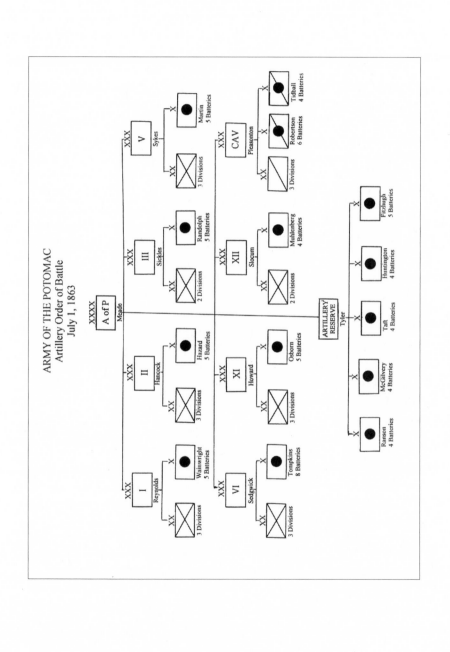

ARMY OF THE POTOMAC
Artillery Order of Battle
July 1, 1863

eight batteries. Guns per brigade ranged from a low of twenty to a high of forty-eight, with an average of twenty-six to twenty-eight. Of the cavalry's two brigades, one had six batteries with thirty guns, and one had four batteries with twenty-two guns. Four of the reserve artillery's brigades had four batteries, with twenty to twenty-four guns in each brigade. A fifth brigade had five batteries with twenty-eight guns.[20]

Hunt's reorganization also eliminated a supply problem. Previously the ammunition supply trains for the artillery were mixed in with the infantry divisions' supply trains. Many times, when a resupply of ammunition was needed, battery personnel could not find their wagons. When the artillery brigade system was instituted, each brigade was provided with its own separate ammunition train that moved under the control of the brigade commander. In addition, there was also a reserve ammunition train under the control of the artillery reserve commander. With direct control of his ammunition train, a brigade commander could have his batteries resupplied, refitted, and back into action at a much faster rate than before. At Gettysburg this capability, in conjunction with the artillery reserve's ammunition train, played a significant role in the effectiveness of the Army of the Potomac's artillery.[21]

There are numerous examples of the effectiveness of this new organization at Gettysburg. On July 1 Colonel Charles Wainwright's First Corps Artillery Brigade and Major Thomas Osborn's Eleventh Corps Artillery Brigade carried the artillery fight. Wainwright attached a battery each to two of the infantry divisions for the march to Gettysburg while keeping the other three under his command. On arriving in the vicinity of Seminary Ridge, he regained control of his two attached batteries and at the same time attached another battery to one of the other infantry divisions. Throughout the rest of the day, Wainwright deployed and fought four of his batteries under his direct command, while a fifth battery remained under the control of the infantry division commander to which it was attached. Similarly, the Eleventh Corps artillery approached Gettysburg with part of its artillery attached to the infantry, while the rest remained under Osborn's control. He initially attached two of his batteries to two of the infantry divisions, while the remaining three remained with him. On reaching the battlefield, he sent one battery to reinforce a battery already in action, deployed another one just behind the center of the corps' battle line, and held the remaining battery in reserve on Cemetery Hill. As the First and Eleventh Corps were pushed off their initial defensive positions and retreated to Cemetery Hill and its vicinity, both artillery commanders brought all of their batteries back under their tactical control. As the artillery positions were consolidated on Cemetery

Hill, it was discovered that the batteries of both corps were intermingled. Wainwright and Osborn solved this potentially disastrous command and control problem by deciding that Osborn would command all of the batteries on Cemetery Hill west of the Baltimore Pike while Wainwright commanded the batteries east of the pike, regardless of which corps they belonged to. As the fighting progressed into July 2 and 3, both Wainwright and Osborn, especially Osborn, were reinforced with additional artillery batteries. Again, any artillery deploying onto West or East Cemetery Hill came under the tactical command of these two artillery officers. This resulted in a concentrated and coordinated use of artillery against Confederate offensive operations on those two days. In addition, Wainwright's ammunition wagons had been misplaced and his batteries were low on ammunition, but he was able to resupply from Osborn's train.[22]

The next day, July 2, Lieutenant Colonel Freeman McGilvery's reserve brigade was used to reinforce Captain George Randolph's Third Corps artillery. Most of McGilvery's guns went into firing positions between the infantry brigades in the Peach Orchard and the Wheatfield. Late in the afternoon a gun from either McGilvery's or Randolph's batteries (but probably one of McGilvery's) did the Union cause excellent service when it wounded Major General John B. Hood. Hood's wounding caused a breakdown in the command and control of his division just as it was commencing its attack against the Union's left. When forced to retreat from the Wheatfield Road position, one of his batteries, the Ninth Massachusetts, delayed part of the Confederate attack long enough for McGilvery to organize a multibattery position on Cemetery Ridge near the George Weikert house at the south end of today's Hancock Avenue. These batteries delayed a potential Confederate breakthrough long enough for infantry reinforcements to arrive and stabilize the position.[23]

The classic example of the effectiveness of the new artillery organization was, of course, on July 3. During the Confederate preattack bombardment, Union artillery provided some counter-battery fire. More important, it was deployed in multiple battery positions, and ammunition was conserved to fire on the attacking infantry. As the Confederate infantry advanced, fresh Union batteries from the reserve were brought into position to relieve or reinforce batteries in the Union center. The fire of the Union artillery was instrumental in producing casualties, thereby reducing the combat power of the attacking infantry.[24]

The acceptance and implementation of Hunt's reforms in the month prior to the campaign created a highly responsive and flexible artillery organization. This timely reorganization provided Meade and his corps commanders a powerful and efficient artillery organization to support the infantry and had a decisive effect on the battle.

The Confederate Cavalry Goes Astray

Prior to the start of the campaign, Major General J. E. B. Stuart's cavalry division was increased in strength from four brigades to six brigades. With a cavalry force of this size, Lee had every expectation that Stuart would be able to provide intelligence on the movements of the Army of the Potomac, thus keeping Lee from being surprised, and also to prevent Union reconnaissance from gaining information on his army.

The missions (roles) of cavalry are reconnaissance, security, and economy-of-force operations. It is that way today, and so it was in 1863. Reconnaissance operations are conducted to gain information about the enemy and the terrain. Security operations are conducted to prevent the enemy from gaining information about the friendly force (sometimes called counter-reconnaissance) and to prevent the friendly force from being surprised by an enemy force. These operations are of three types: guard missions, screen missions, and covering-force operations. A guard mission is preformed close to the friendly main body and is characterized as advance guard, rear guard, or flank guard depending where the cavalry is deployed in relationship to the main body. A cavalry force conducting a guard mission will fight to protect the main body or conduct a delay to gain time for the main body to deploy on favorable terrain and prepare for combat. The screen mission is done instead of the guard mission when the cavalry has insufficient force or must cover a very large front or flank. The screen mission is an observation-and-report type of operation. The covering-force missions are the same as the guard missions, only the cavalry force is operating out of supporting distance of the force it is protecting. An economy-of-force operation is any tactical operation where a cavalry unit is used to allow other combat forces to be deployed to another location. For example, a cavalry force may hold a section of a defensive line to allow the infantry and armor units that were there to be moved into position to add more weight to a main attack. This is just what Lee did on the first day of the Seven Days, when he held the area in front of Richmond and sent units to the area of Beaver Dam Creek to join with Jackson for an attack on the Union right flank. Lee in this case used infantry and some cavalry as the economy-of-force units.[25]

An 1859 West Point graduate, Stuart had commanded Lee's cavalry since the summer of 1862. His first major operation for Lee had been the famous "Ride Around McClellan" that provided vital information for Lee's planning for the Seven Days. Since then he had participated in all the Army of Northern Virginia's battles, where his cavalry consistently excelled in performing their traditional roles.[26]

On the eve of the Gettysburg Campaign, Stuart, surprised by Union cavalry at Brandy Station, rallied his forces and fought a credible action. This combat was followed from June 17 to June 21 in the fighting around Aldie, Middleburg, and Upperville. There the Union cavalry fought to penetrate Stuart's flank guard positions in order to gain information on the location of Lee's army. Throughout this extended action, Stuart was able to block each Union at-

Major General J. E. B. Stuart. U.S. Army Military History Institute.

tempt and to protect the exact location of the Army of Northern Virginia as it moved north in the Shenandoah Valley. Stuart started the campaign in the same exemplary fashion that he had demonstrated in the past. It was not to continue.[27]

On June 22 and 23 Stuart received messages that provided directions for his cavalry to cross the Potomac River and take position on the right of Ewell's Corps. A message from Lee to Stuart on June 23 provided the most detailed instructions. It contained this discretionary paragraph: "If General Hooker's army remains inactive, you can leave two brigades to watch him, and withdraw with the three others, but should he not appear to be moving northward, I think you had better withdraw this side of the mountain to-morrow night, cross at Shepherdstown [west of the mountains] next day, and move over to Fredericktown [Frederick, Maryland]. You will, however, be able to judge whether you *can pass around their army without hinderance* [emphasis added], doing them all the damage you can, and cross the river east of the mountains. In either case, after crossing the river, you must move on and feel [take position on] the right of Ewell's troops, collecting information, provisions, &c." Note the qualifying phrase in italics.[28]

Lee's message did not order Stuart to pass (ride) around the Army of the Potomac. Lee provided Stuart with two courses of actions from which to choose. He could cross the Potomac River west of the Blue Ridge Mountains or cross the river east of the mountains after passing around the Union army. In either option the cavalry was then to take position on Ewell's flank. Once there Stuart could conduct a flank guard operation. However, Lee did place a qualifier in his message. Stuart could pass around the Union army if he did not encounter any "hinderance," that is, serious opposition.

Stuart left three of his six brigades behind. Two were ordered to cover the gaps in the Blue Ridge Mountains to prevent a Union force from moving west undetected and taking position across Lee's line of communication. One was attached to Ewell's Corps to assist his movement north in the Cumberland Valley. A seventh independent brigade was operating to the west of Lee's advance and gathering food and forage. With the other three brigades, on June 25 he commenced his operation to move around the Army of the Potomac. Almost immediately Stuart made contact with the Union Second Corps in the vicinity of Haymarket, Virginia. Unable to get through the Second Corps, he detoured farther south to pass behind them and continued on east. Contact with the Second Corps in such strength that he had to detour south was a certainly a "hinderance." Most of his fighting to protect the gaps in the Bull Run Mountains had been against cavalry. However, once he made contact with a large infantry force, Stuart had the information to begin developing the intelligence as to the location of the Army of the Potomac.[29]

An experienced commander, Stuart, once he made contact with such strong opposition as the Second Corps, should have realized that his only option, as Lee stipulated, was to cancel his move around the Union army and to cross the Potomac River west of the mountains. After crossing he would have been in position to conduct reconnaissance and flank guard operations. These operations could have provided intelligence on the positions and movements of the Union army and protect Lee's, and especially Ewell's, right flank. Protection of his flank as his army advanced north, not a raid around the Army of the Potomac, was Lee's primary mission for his cavalry. It is interesting to note that Stuart did send a message to Lee about his contact with the Second Corps, but it never made it to Lee's headquarters.

However, Stuart decided to continue on and disappeared to the east with three cavalry brigades. Stuart and his three brigades did not rejoin the army until July 2 at Gettysburg. The eight days Stuart was absent had denied Lee the vital use of half the cavalry.

Although there were other cavalry brigades with his army, Lee apparently never issued orders for them to take position on Ewell's or the army's right flank. Placed in such a position, they could have provided the reconnaissance needed to determine the Army of the Potomac's location and prevent Lee from being surprised. The consequences of Stuart's decision and Lee's failure to redeploy the remaining cavalry to his right flank were severe and far-reaching.

First, Lee was not sure where the Army of the Potomac was located. In a letter to Jefferson Davis on June 23, Lee wrote that he thought a pontoon bridge was laid at Edwards Ferry and the Army of the Potomac was preparing to cross the Potomac River. However, believing they were preparing to cross the river and knowing they were crossing or had crossed are two different things. He could reasonably expect that his cavalry would provide him with that information once a crossing had occurred. In the absence of such information, he must have assumed the crossing had not taken place. At Chambersburg, Pennsylvania, on the night of June 28, Lee was surprised when he received information that the Union army was in the vicinity of Frederick, Maryland, just fifty-eight road miles away.[30]

During a conversation with William Allen in 1868, Lee remarked that he did not know the Army of the Potomac was at Gettysburg. Stuart had been ordered to cover Lee's movement and to keep him informed of Meade's locations. The lack of that information meant Lee was unprepared for the proximity of the Union army to his army.[31]

In his report Lee wrote that "Preparations had been made to advance on Harrisburg, [Pennsylvania.]." Charles Marshall, one of Lee's staff officers, elaborated on this almost buried phrase. Marshall wrote that, in the absence of information from Stuart, Lee believed the Army of the Potomac was south of the Potomac River and still in Virginia. In order to force it to cross the river, he had Marshall prepare and distribute orders on June 28 to the three corps commanders. Ewell, who had two divisions at Carlisle and one at York, was ordered to advance directly on Harrisburg. Longstreet was to march his corps north from Chambersburg on the twenty-ninth to support Ewell. Hill was directed to move directly east from Chambersburg to the Susquehanna River, cross the river, and seize the railroad between Harrisburg and Philadelphia. These orders are not the ones that would have been issued if Lee had known the Union army was north of the Potomac and approaching his army. Although Ewell and Longstreet would be concentrated in the Carlisle-Harrisburg area, Hill's Corps would be on its own and out of supporting distance. In addition, in marching from Chambersburg to the Susquehanna River, Hill would be moving directly across the Army of the Potomac's marching routes north and in a precarious position to be overwhelmingly attacked in the flank.[32]

On the night of June 28, Lee received vital information from a scout, Henry Thomas Harrison, employed by Longstreet. Harrison informed Lee that the Union army was north of the Potomac River in the vicinity of Frederick, Maryland. Until this time Lee had thought his adversary might still be south of the river. Believing that the Army of the Potomac was farther away than it was, Lee had allowed his army to become extended in the Cumberland Valley. There was a distinct possibility that Major General George G. Meade (by then commanding the Union army) could separately engage Lee's spread-out army and defeat it piecemeal. Lee immediately rescinded the orders that had gone out earlier and instructed his corps commanders to concentrate in the Cashtown-Gettysburg area. This order would bring the Union and Confederate armies to battle in the area around Gettysburg.[33]

Second, on June 30 Pettigrew's infantry brigade of Heth's Division from Hill's Corps was sent east from Cashtown to Gettysburg to search for supplies. On reaching the ridges west of the town, the troops saw a cavalry force at Gettysburg. Pettigrew withdrew back toward Cashtown, where he reported that he had seen elements of the Army of the Potomac at Gettysburg. Neither Heth nor Hill, who thought Pettigrew had seen local militia who would not offer an effective resistance, believed this information. The next day, July 1, Heth marched his four-brigade infantry division toward Gettysburg to determine what was there and ran directly into Buford's cavalry and then elements of the Army of the Potomac's First Corps. On making contact, Heth ordered two of his infantry brigades, supported by his other two, to deploy, advance, and conduct a reconnaissance in force. The infantry were performing the reconnaissance mission of cavalry. Had Stuart's cavalry been in the proper location, Pettigrew would not have been sent toward Gettysburg on June 30, and Heth would not have stumbled into a fight on July 1 for which he was not prepared. Instead, part of Stuart's cavalry would have been deployed in the vicinity of Cashtown, or even Gettysburg, to protect the pass through South Mountain and to gain information. This force would have made contact with Buford's cavalry as it came to Gettysburg, if it had not already done so. That contact would have produced information that part of the cavalry of the Army of the Potomac, not militia, was at Gettysburg. The presence of its cavalry at Gettysburg should have led to the conclusion that the Army of the Potomac was not far away. Instead of withdrawing as the infantry did, the Confederate cavalry could have maintained an observation and guarding position while it continued to gain information and provide a protected position for Hill's Corps to deploy behind when the decision to attack or defend was made.[34]

Third, improper use of the cavalry attached to Ewell's Corps on the afternoon of July 1 helped to prevent him from pushing his attack to a total victory by assaulting Cemetery Hill. Ewell had two of his three divisions in the battle on July 1. The third did not arrive until almost dark. One of his divisions, Rodes's, was disorganized and temporarily reduced in combat effectiveness by the fighting. The other division, Early's, had taken fewer casualties and was still a powerful force. But two of its infantry brigades were sent off a short distance to the east of Gettysburg when a report was received of a Union force approaching from that direction. This reduced by half the force Ewell and Early had to attack Cemetery Hill. Again the correct deployment of cavalry on Ewell's flank could have kept him informed of any enemy force's approach and size. This would have given Ewell four brigades on July 1, rather than two, to attack Cemetery Hill, if he chose to do so.

Last, on the morning of July 2, Lee was faced with the decision as to what course of action he should adopt: defend or attack and if attack, where and with whom? Because of the fighting the previous day, he had fairly good information about the Union position around Culp's Hill and Cemetery Hill. However, his information concerning the area south to the Round Tops, such as character of the ground, concealed routes of movement, and enemy forces present, was lacking. An attempt was made by staff officers to gather as much information as possible, but as we now know this attempt produced little information and, even worse, incorrect information.

Lee's plan for Longstreet's attack on July 2 was based on faulty information as to the location of Meade's defensive position. Cavalry could have provided the reconnaissance and information Lee needed to formulate his plans. In addition, a cavalry force operating on Lee's right flank could have kept observation over the area while Longstreet marched to his attack positions. This cavalry could have observed the movement of the Union Third Corps to the Peach Orchard and Emmitsburg Road. Providing this information to Longstreet would have prevented the surprise that awaited him and his division commanders. Such information could have resulted in a different deployment by Longstreet's Corps.

A good example of how cavalry could have aided Lee and Longstreet on July 2 can be found two months earlier, on May 2, 1863, at the Battle of Chancellorsville. On that day Jackson was marching his command from generally in front of the Union left to a position on the Union right flank for the purpose of conducting a flank attack. Supporting his move was Fitz-Hugh Lee's four-regiment cavalry brigade. As Jackson marched southwest and then northwest, cavalry units blocked roads and trails that intercepted his route of march. That was a flank guard operation. Preceding his march was an advance guard of cavalry. When Jackson reached the Orange Plank Road, he expected to turn northeast (right) and be on the flank of the Union Eleventh Corps, which was the army's right-most corps. The cavalry advanced guard discovered that if Jackson turned when he planned, he would not be on the Union right flank but would be conducting a front attack against the Eleventh Corps rather than a flank attack. Jackson immediately extended his march farther northwest and, when he came to the Orange Turnpike, turned right, deployed, and attacked the Union right flank with devastating results. It is very easy to project this scenario, given cavalry, to Longstreet's Corps as it marched for what it thought was the Union left flank on July 2.[35]

CHAPTER 2

WEDNESDAY, JULY 1, 1863

Lee began redeploying his army away from Fredericksburg, Virginia, on June 3 and concentrating near Culpepper. One week later he sent Ewell's Corps into the Shenandoah Valley, and the rest of his army followed shortly thereafter. Winchester was captured on June 14, and the next day the lead units of the army crossed the Potomac River into Maryland. The Gettysburg Campaign was underway. On June 26 the last units of Lee's army crossed into Maryland while fifty miles downriver the Army of the Potomac did the same. Both armies were now moving northeast on either side of the eighty-mile-long South Mountain. On June 28 Ewell's Corps was in the vicinity of Carlisle and York, Pennsylvania. The rest of Lee's army, except for the cavalry, was near Chambersburg. That night Lee received information that the Union army, which he thought might still be south of the Potomac River, was in Maryland and moving north. He immediately ordered his army to concentrate in the Cashtown-Gettysburg area, but not to bring on a general engagement until the army was concentrated. The next day Ewell started his corps south while A. P. Hill began moving his corps east through South Mountain to Cashtown.[1]

Buford Conducts a Delaying Action

Brigadier General John Buford's decision to control key terrain at Gettysburg with a delaying action and Major General John Reynolds's decision to move forward and reinforce Buford are actually two separate decisions. However, because of the symbiotic relationship between them, they must be considered together.

On graduating from West Point in 1848, John Buford was assigned to the Second Dragoons and served with his regiment on the western frontier prior to the Civil War. Promoted to brigadier general in July 1862, he commanded a cavalry brigade during the Second Bull Run Campaign and then was chief of cavalry for the Army of the Potomac during the 1862 Maryland Campaign and at the Battle of Fredericksburg. He then returned to brigade command and shortly thereafter was given command of a cavalry division.[2]

Brigadier General John Buford. Library of Congress.

Buford's cavalry division was deployed on the Army of the Potomac's left flank as it moved north into Maryland and toward Pennsylvania. As the army moved, Buford conducted reconnaissance and guard operations. These operations were to accomplish two missions, gain information on the location and movements of Lee's army and protect Meade from a surprise attack.[3]

On June 30 John Reynolds, who was the First Corps commander, and Buford met briefly at Emmitsburg. Buford's division had just come from the vicinity of Fairfield, to the west of Emmitsburg, where it had been in contact with Confederate infantry. Realizing that contact with Lee's army would probably occur within the next twenty-four to forty-eight hours, these two experienced commanders would not have passed up the opportunity to coordinate what actions they might take when that occurred.[4]

Departing Emmetsburg, Buford arrived at Gettysburg that afternoon. As Buford's division approached Gettysburg, the advance guard reported Confederate troops withdrawing west along the Chambersburg Pike. This was a part of Pettigrew's Brigade that had been sent in advance of Hill's Corps to gather supplies in Gettysburg and conduct a reconnaissance of the area, a mission normally done by cavalry.[5]

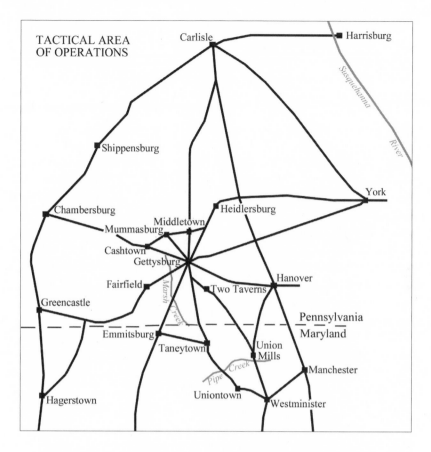

TACTICAL AREA
OF OPERATIONS

Carlisle

Harrisburg

Susquehanna

River

Shippensburg

York

Chambersburg
Heidlersburg
Middletown
Mummasburg
Cashtown
Gettysburg
Fairfield
Hanover
Two Taverns
Greencastle

Marsh Creek

Pennsylvania
Maryland

Emmitsburg
Taneytown
Union Mills
Manchester

Pipe Creek

Hagerstown
Uniontown
Westminister

Deploying his division in and around Gettysburg, Buford sent out patrols and questioned civilians in the area. By late evening he had developed an accurate estimate as to the locations of the Confederate army and determined it was moving toward Gettysburg from the west and north. In two messages, one written at 10:30 and the other at 10:40 P.M., Buford passed this intelligence to the Cavalry Corps commander and the commander of the nearest infantry, John Reynolds.[6]

By nightfall, June 30, the Union infantry was in positions from which it could begin to arrive at Buford's location in two to three hours, or if the situation dictated, Buford could easily fall back to the infantry. Reynolds's corps had moved to where the Gettysburg-Emmitsburg Road crosses Marsh Creek, and it was only eight miles from Buford. Oliver O. Howard's Eleventh Corps was at Emmitsburg, thirteen miles from Buford, and Daniel Sickles's Third Corps was fifteen miles away. All these corps were under Reynolds's tactical command.[7]

Key terrain is terrain that provides an advantage to whoever occupies or controls it. To control key terrain, it is not necessary to occupy it physically but only to prevent the enemy from occupying or controlling it. John Buford identified the key terrain at Gettysburg. First among them were the roads that came into and left Gettysburg from all directions of the compass. Control of these roads provided a commander the capability to concentrate his army in the Gettysburg area or to move on many strategic objectives, such as Harrisburg, Baltimore, and even Washington. The high ground west of town—Seminary Ridge, McPherson's Ridge, and Oak Ridge—provided a defending force the capability to block enemy movement toward Gettysburg from the west. Conversely, control of that terrain by a force marching on roads from the west facilitated movement to Gettysburg, provided positions from which to conduct offensive operation toward the north or to the south of Gettysburg, and protected the routes of supply and communication. The high ground south of the town, Culp's Hill and Cemetery Hill, controlled the roads to the south and southeast. Control of this terrain blocked any force maneuvering south or southeast from Gettysburg. Conversely, it facilitated the movement and became the supply route of any force marching to Gettysburg from the south and southeast. There is other key terrain in the Gettysburg area, but it was not necessary to control it for Buford's purpose.[8]

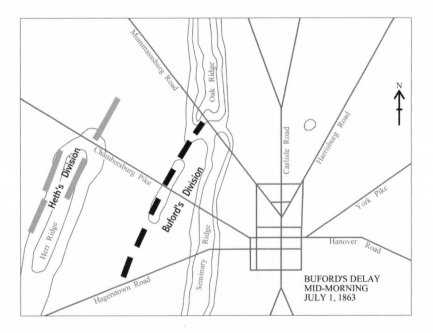

BUFORD'S DELAY
MID-MORNING
JULY 1, 1863

Seeing the advantages of the terrain around Gettysburg as a potential battlefield, Buford decided to conduct a delaying action. This is used to impede the movement of a much larger force. The units conducting the delay deploy forward of key terrain and fight a series of engagements to cause the enemy force to deploy into attack formations. The delaying force holds their position for as long as possible, without becoming decisively engaged, and then withdraws to the next terrain feature where the action sequence is repeated. Essentially the delaying force is trading space for time. The time gained allows other friendly forces to deploy behind the delaying force or to move forward and reinforce. Recognizing the importance of Gettysburg and the surrounding terrain, Buford decided that he would fight a delaying action to gain time for the infantry to march to Gettysburg.[9]

Since for his purpose the key terrain was the road network radiating from Gettysburg, the ridges west of town, and the commanding hills south and southeast of the town, he deployed his force west and north of the town. Buford's delaying action provided the Union corps marching toward him the options of establishing battle positions on the key terrain west of the town or on the key terrain to the south and southeast. It also provided Buford with the ability to give up ground if necessary and still protect some of the key terrain. Buford's decision began a sequence of events that brought the armies

The center of Buford's position on McPherson's Ridge, as seen from Seminary Ridge. The road in the right of the photograph is the Chambersburg Pike. The McPherson Barn is the building in the center of the photo.

into battle at Gettysburg. His masterful delaying action west of the town forced the lead division of Hill's Corps—Heth's Division—into the time-consuming act of having to deploying on both sides of the Chambersburg Pike. At the same time, his cavalry to the north discovered Ewell's movements and provided information on the threat developing there.[10]

If Buford had not chosen to delay the Confederate advance west of Gettysburg, the battle would have been fought on different terrain. Without Buford's delaying action, divisions from Hill's Corps, and perhaps Ewell's Corps, would have occupied the key terrain and the roads west and north, and perhaps even south and southeast, of Gettysburg. This would have changed the complete orientation of both armies on July 1 and the days following.

Reynolds Reinforces Buford

Buford's decision by itself would not have brought any results unless it was backed up with another decision. For Buford's actions to have meaning, they required a follow-up decision to bring the Army of the Potomac to where he was. The closest infantry commander was Major General John Reynolds. Normally the First Corps Commander, he was temporarily commanding

three corps of the army's left wing. This gave him tactical control of First, Third, and Eleventh Corps.[11]

A veteran of the Mexican War, where he served in Braxton Bragg's Battery E, Third U.S. Artillery, with Daniel H. Hill and George H. Thomas, Reynolds at the outbreak of the Civil War was commandant of cadets at West Point. Promoted to brigadier general of volunteers in 1861 and to major general in November 1862, he participated in the Peninsula Campaign, Second Bull Run, Fredericksburg, and Chancellorsville, the last as a corps commander. At the commencement of the Gettysburg

Major General John F. Reynolds. Library of Congress.

Campaign, he was one of the most aggressive and competent commanders in the Army of the Potomac.[12]

By June 30 Meade had received sufficient information as to Lee's movements and dispositions that he could conceptualize that the armies might come into action in the vicinity of Gettysburg. With that in mind, on that day he ordered Reynolds to proceed in the direction of Gettysburg. Because the situation was still developing, he allowed Reynolds some latitude with his instructions. Meade also issued to his army what today is called a warning order. This order provided the corps commanders with Meade's assessment that Lee's army was apparently moving toward Gettysburg. Commanders were ordered to be prepared to march against the enemy at a moment's notice. In anticipation of a coming battle, supply trains, except for ammunition wagons, were ordered to the rear. Each soldier was to have on his person sixty rounds of ammunition, a sure indicator that a fight was expected.[13]

Orders were issued late on June 30 for the movement of the army on July 1. The First Corps, with the Eleventh Corps following in a supporting role, was ordered to Gettysburg.[14]

Late on the night of June 30, Reynolds received a message from Buford at Gettysburg. This message provided him with the intelligence that Hill's Corps was located at Cashtown, about nine miles from Gettysburg, Longstreet's Corps was behind Hill's on the road from Chambersburg to Gettysburg, and Ewell's Corps was en route from Carlisle. For Reynolds, Buford's message would have reinforced Meade's assessment of Lee's intentions to concentrate in the vicinity of Gettysburg.[15]

On July 1 Reynolds had Brigadier General James S. Wadsworth's division on the road to Gettysburg at 8:00 A.M., with the rest of the First Corps following a short time afterward. Howard also began marching his Eleventh Corps toward Gettysburg at 8:00 A.M. Reynolds and his staff marched with and then ahead of Wadsworth's division. As Reynolds approached Gettysburg on the Emmitsburg Road, a messenger from Buford gave Reynolds a note that informed him the cavalry was heavily engaged. Reynolds immediately continued on and found Buford in action on the ridges west of the town. There Buford briefed him on the tactical situation.[16]

Reynolds had three possible courses of action from which to choose. First, he could order the corps of the left wing into a defensive position on terrain south of Emmitsburg, an area that had earlier been considered. It would have been difficult to implement this course of action as the divisions of both corps were already on the march and many of them were already north of Emmitsburg. Second, Buford could continue his delay as long as possible while the infantry went into position on the key terrain south and southeast of Gettysburg. This was a viable course of action that occupied key terrain protecting the routes of advance Meade could use to deploy the remainder of the army forward. Third, Reynolds could continue moving his infantry forward, conduct a relief in place, take over Buford's positions, transition from the delay to the defense, and continue the fight. This course of action, if successful, had the advantages of fighting on key terrain west of Gettysburg, protecting the army's routes of advance and providing Meade the options of deploying west or south-southeast of Gettysburg. Reynolds chose the third course of action.

Having made his decision, he immediately sent staff officers to hurry up the march of the First and Eleventh Corps. Reynolds then sent Captain Stephen Weld of his staff to Meade. Ordered to ride as fast as possible, even if it killed his horse, he was to inform Meade that the enemy forces were advancing on Gettysburg in strength and that Reynolds was concerned about controlling the terrain west of Gettysburg but would hold as long as possible. Returning to the Emmitsburg Road, Reynolds ordered Wadsworth's Division to march cross-country to Buford's position. Reynolds then returned to McPherson's Ridge and shortly thereafter was killed.[17]

Reynolds's death on July 1 precluded his writing an after-action report for the *Official Records,* postbattle letters, a memoir, or articles for any number of journals and papers after the war. Because of his death, we may never fully know Reynolds's thoughts and decision-making process when he decided to move forward to reinforce Buford and brought a battle to the peaceful rural town of Gettysburg. However, we do have some indirect and circumstantial evidence that gives us clues.

Earlier in June, as the army was marching north, Reynolds told one of his division commanders that he was "most of getting at the enemy" and that "it was necessary to attack the enemy at once to prevent them from plundering the whole state," meaning his home state of Pennsylvania. This indicates his state of mind and an aggressive tendency to close with the invading Confederate army.[18]

On June 30 Reynolds received an order for him to assume command of three corps, First, Third, and Eleventh, which formed the army's left wing. This was a temporary command and control measure designed to reduce Meade's span of control and provide for more efficient maneuver and battle management. However, it provided Reynolds with direct tactical command of three of the army's seven corps. This was a force sufficient to engage part or all of Lee's army for a short period of time while the remainder of the army marched to reinforce him.[19]

That same day Reynolds and Buford had a brief meeting at Emmitsburg. Buford's division had just come from the vicinity of Fairfield, to the west of

Emmitsburg, where it had been in contact with Confederate infantry. Given that contact with Lee's army seemed likely within the next twenty-four to forty-eight hours, it is highly possible that they would have taken this opportunity to coordinate what actions they might take when that occurred. Later that night, Reynolds received an intelligence report from Buford at Gettysburg informing him that parts of Lee's army were close to Gettysburg and advancing on that location. Also, he had received orders to march his corps on July 1 to Gettysburg and for the Eleventh Corps also to march to Gettysburg or within supporting distance of the First Corps.[20]

In the early morning hours of July 1, Meade's headquarters issued a circular that detailed a contingency plan to defend, if necessary, along Pipe Creek, a situation that will be examined later. Reynolds never received this circular, or if he did, he realized it was overcome by events.[21]

On the morning of July 1, Reynolds was marching his command toward Gettysburg as ordered, and he had information that part of Lee's army was in that vicinity. He also had tactical command of a significant force, he believed that the Confederates must be engaged in order to stop the "plundering" of his home state, and he had no information concerning a contingency plan that would have provided him the option to fall back if necessary. All these conditions would lead an aggressive and competent commander to do what Reynolds did. He moved forward to engage the enemy.

Reynolds's decision began the sequence of events that initiated the combat between the advance corps of both armies. It would subsequently bring the remainder of both armies into battle at Gettysburg.

If Reynolds had not made the decision to move forward, then, except for Buford's delaying action, there would not have been any major combat on July 1. Union infantry would not have occupied and fought on the terrain west and north of Gettysburg. It is possible they would not have occupied Cemetery Hill or Culp's Hill. The entire orientations, positions, and tactical situations of both armies would have been different. The Battle of Gettysburg as we know it would not have occurred.

Ewell and Rodes Decide to Attack Immediately on Arriving North of Gettysburg

On the night of June 28 a scout/spy, Henry Harrison, informed Lee that the Army of the Potomac had crossed the Potomac River and was marching north. Lee immediately canceled his previous orders for an advance on Harrisburg and issued an order for his army to concentrate in the Gettysburg-Cashtown area. At that time Lieutenant General Richard S. Ewell's Second Corps was in the vicinity of Carlisle and York, twenty-six miles north and thirty-two miles northeast of Gettysburg. Lieutenant General A. P. Hill's Third Corps and Lieutenant General James Longstreet's First Corps were twenty-four miles west of Gettysburg. By nightfall on June 30, Hill's Corps was in the vicinity of Cashtown, Longstreet's Corps was behind Hill's, and Ewell's Corps was northeast of Gettysburg.[22]

Early on the morning of July 1, Hill ordered Heth to march his division toward Gettysburg to discover what was in front of his troops. Again, infantry was performing a cavalry mission. Heth's Division made contact with Buford's cavalry west of McPherson's Ridge at about 8:00 A.M. He deployed his division and commenced a reconnaissance in force. That same day Ewell's Corps had been marching to rejoin the army.[23]

On July 28 Ewell's Corps was at Carlisle (Rodes's and Johnson's Divisions) and York (Early's Division) with a brigade on the Susquehanna River at Wrightsville. Ewell was preparing to concentrate his corps, maneuver to cross the Susquehanna River, and capture Harrisburg. Lee's order to concentrate the army in the Cashtown-Gettysburg area changed Ewell's plans. His three divisions marched toward Cashtown over three separate routes. One division and the corps reserve artillery battalions were separated from the rest of the corps by South Mountain. This was not the tactical disposition a corps commander would make if he thought a battle was imminent.[24]

Major General Robert E. Rodes's division marched south from Carlisle on June 30 and by evening had traveled twenty-two miles to Heidlersburg, ten miles northeast of Gettysburg, where it spent the night. Departing York, Major General Jubal A. Early's division marched nineteen miles and camped three miles east of Heidlersburg. Ewell's third division (Major General Edward Johnson's) and the reserve artillery left Carlisle, retraced their route of advance in the Cumberland Valley, and marched twenty-six miles to Green Village (Greenville), just north of Chambersburg. Johnson's route placed South Mountain between his division and the rest of Ewell's Corps. The following day Johnson marched his division east through South Mountain toward Gettysburg. Entangled with Longstreet's Corps, it did not arrive until evening, when the first day's fighting was over.[25]

On July 1 Rodes's and Early's Divisions initially marched from Heidlersburg toward Cashtown. Rodes marched his division west from Heidlersburg, with the intention of passing through Middletown (today's Biglerville) and continuing on west and southwest through Mummasburg to Cashtown. Early's Division marched to Heidlersburg, where it turned southwest, intending to march south four miles toward Gettysburg and intersect with a road to Mummasburg and Cashtown. Ewell's intention was for both divisions to pass north of Gettysburg on their way to Cashtown. With Ewell moving west and Hill and Longstreet marching east, by evening Lee would have had his army concentrated in the vicinity of Cashtown. What happened next began a series of events that led to a decision which changed everything.[26]

Shortly after the time when Heth's Division made the initial contact with Buford's cavalry, Rodes's Division was seven miles north of Gettysburg at Middletown. Rodes's Division was marching in a westerly direction toward Cashtown when Ewell received word from Hill that he was moving on Gettysburg. Ewell may have also heard the cannon fire on McPherson's Ridge. At Middletown he turned Rodes south and ordered Major General Jubal Early, whose division was moving on a separate route for Cashtown, also to march to Gettysburg. After receiving this order, Early continued to march on the Heidlersburg Road, rather than turn off toward Mummasburg and Cashtown, and approached Gettysburg from the northeast. Ewell now had two of his divisions approaching Gettysburg: Rodes's from the north and Early's from the northeast.[27]

Ewell informed Lee, who at this time was approximately fourteen miles west of Gettysburg, of his change in direction. In acknowledging Ewell's communication, Lee sent a message telling him that "he [Lee] did not want a general engagement brought on till the rest of the army came up." These instructions along with others issued earlier clearly show Lee's intentions. While he was prepared to fully engage the Union army, his intention was to use July 1 to bring his army together. Then, from a position of strength he would attack or maneuver against the Army of the Potomac.[28]

Robert Rodes was a veteran combat commander. He began the war as colonel of the Fifth Alabama Infantry and led his regiment at the First Battle of Bull Run. Promoted to brigadier general in late 1861 and then to major general in May 1863, he had participated as a brigade or division commander in every major battle and campaign of the Army of Northern Virginia.[29]

Major General Robert E. Rodes. U.S. Army Military History Institute.

The Union First Corps position as Rodes viewed it. Rodes incorrectly thought the flank of the First Corps was in the trees in the left center of the photograph. McPherson's Barn is next to the trees in the right center of the photograph. The right and center of Rodes's Division attacked forward, across the open field, from the position where this photo was taken.

Following Ewell's orders, when his division reached the intersection of the east-west and north-south roads in Middletown, Rodes turned it left (south). As his division marched south toward Gettysburg, he deployed the lead brigade. His division then moved off the road to the west and continued south on a wooded ridgeline, continuing to deploy as it moved. When his division came out of the woods, it was centered on Oak Ridge (also called Oak Hill), a northern extension of Seminary Ridge. Until this point only one division, Heth's, of Lee's army had been committed to battle. It was still not too late to withdraw Heth to a temporary defensive position on Herr Ridge, deploy skirmishers to maintain contact, develop the situation, and cover the arrival of the rest of the army. Concurrently, Pender's Division could have deployed forward to support Heth while Rodes and Early were held in covered positions north of Gettysburg.[30]

When he reached Oak Hill, Rodes saw that he was on the flank of the Union First Corps. This was also the intersection of the First and Eleventh Corps battle lines, which were at an approximate right angle to each other. Rodes immediately, with Ewell's concurrence, launched an attack. This attack failed, but it had the effect of bringing Early's Division into the battle.[31]

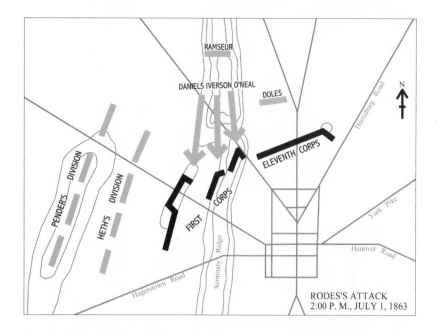

RODES'S ATTACK
2:00 P. M., JULY 1, 1863

Early's Division arrived from the northeast and deployed to a position on Rodes's left. This positioned Early to strike the right flank of the Eleventh Corps, which was located on a small knoll (today called Barlow's Knoll). This attack, along with a renewal of Rodes's attack and the commitment of Pender's Division from Hill's Corps, drove the two Union Corps off their positions west and north of Gettysburg.[32]

This final attack was ordered by Lee shortly after he had arrived on the field and had found a majority of the Confederate forces then close to Gettysburg already engaged in a battle that he was not yet ready to fight. The catalyst that brought on this general engagement was Rodes's decision to attack. When Rodes attacked, he brought Early's Division, the remainder of Heth's Division, and Pender's Division into the fight.[33]

Contrary to Lee's instructions, by mid-afternoon almost one-half of his army had been decisively committed to a battle at Gettysburg. It is not that Lee did not want to fight at Gettysburg; he was prepared to fight the Army of the Potomac when he had his army concentrated. This concentration would have occurred the evening of July 1 or the morning of July 2. With all of his corps in close proximity to each other, Lee could have attacked or defended from a position of strength. The fighting on the first day created such heavy casualties in three of his divisions that they were of marginal strength for further offensive operations. This caused a piecemeal commitment of the

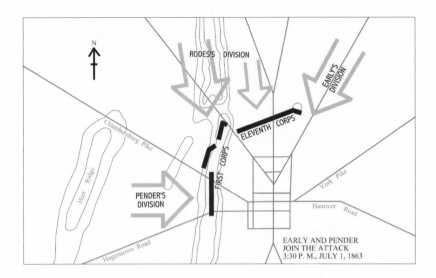

remaining divisions as they arrived on the battlefield, and it also prevented Lee from developing and deploying the full combat power of his army at a decisive point. It had a direct effect on how Lee's army was positioned and how he fought it on July 2.

Ewell Decides Not to Attack Cemetery Hill

Several decisions made at Gettysburg became very controversial and damaging to the reputation of the person responsible. This is one of them. However, if we examine the decision from Ewell's perspective, we gain some insights into why he made the decision he did.

This was Ewell's first campaign as a corps commander. A soldier all of his adult life, he spent the twenty-one years prior to the war in the southwestern territories. Resigning his U.S. Army commission in May 1861, he was commissioned a brigadier general in the Confederate army, and the next year promoted to major general. A brigade commander at First Bull Run, he commanded a division in the Valley Campaign, the Seven Days, and Second Bull Run, where he was wounded and had his left leg amputated above the knee. In the reorganization of Lee's army, he was promoted to lieutenant general and given command of a corps.[34]

Late in the afternoon of July 1, the combined attacks of Hill's and Ewell's two corps had driven the Union First and Eleventh Corps off their initial defensive positions and back through Gettysburg to the key terrain of Cemetery Hill. Seeing this success, Lee instructed Ewell "to carry the hill [Cemetery Hill] occupied by the enemy, if he found it practicable, but to avoid a general engagement until the arrival of other divisions of the army."[35]

Any commander would, when issued a combat order, require some essential elements of information to go forward. What is the mission, and what is the commander's intent? What is the enemy situation, and where are his troops? What is the friendly situation, and what friendly troops are available? When Ewell received Lee's ambiguous order, he might have asked himself: "What is Lee's intent?" "What does practicable mean?" "Take the hill if I meet no resistance, or use whatever units of my

Lieutenant General Richard S. Ewell. National Archives.

corps are available in a fight for the hill?" "And how can this be done without bringing on a general engagement?" In Ewell's mind there surely was some doubt as to how the order to "carry [capture] the hill" balanced with Lee's stated intention "to avoid a general engagement."

As for the Union situation, Ewell would have known there were two Union corps and possibly a cavalry division at Gettysburg. From captured soldiers he may have even known the corps were the First and Eleventh. He had seen them retreat through the town and could see what was left of these two corps move to positions on Cemetery Hill. He may even have seen the infantry brigade and artillery battery that had remained on the hill when the rest of the Eleventh Corps had been committed to the fight. Both corps used this brigade as an anchor to establish new defensive positions. Certainly he saw the majority of the corps artillery brigades—some eight batteries, plus the one left there—as they moved up the hill and into firing positions. In addition, Ewell had received a report of Union troops somewhere off to the east along the York Pike. The type and size of this force were unknown, but, if large enough, it could strike the flank of any Confederate attack on Cemetery Hill. Although the report was in error, Ewell did not know it at the time.[36]

When Ewell began to survey the available friendly troops, the situation was far from promising. Ewell had three divisions in his corps. One division, commanded by Major General Edward Johnson, was separated from the corps when it marched back down the Cumberland Valley from Carlisle. On July 1 it marched toward Gettysburg on the Chambersburg Pike and arrived at dark, about 8:13 P.M., and was not available that day for an attack. The remaining two divisions were at Gettysburg. Rodes's Division had taken significant casualties and was incapable of further action that day. As a unit this division would not participate in any major fighting on July 2 or 3. Only Early's Division was available to continue the attack. The division's four brigades had conducted the attack against the Eleventh Corps' right flank. After the Eleventh Corps retreated through Gettysburg, two of Early's brigades had been sent two miles to the east to protect against the suspected Union threat coming down the York Pike. Ewell had sent Captain James P. Smith of his staff to find Lee and ask for a force to attack on his right as he attacked Cemetery Hill. Smith returned with the message that Lee had no troops to support Ewell. Ewell was on his own. If an attack were to be conducted, it would have to be done with just two brigades.[37]

Many have assumed that Cemetery Hill was Ewell's for the taking. But the position was stronger than it initially appeared, and it became stronger as time went by. When the Eleventh Corps marched through town to its initial positions, Colonel Orlando Smith's four-regiment brigade and Captain Michael Wiedrich's six-gun battery were left in position on Cemetery Hill.

Gettysburg as seen from the northern part of Oak Ridge. Cemetery Hill is the wooded high ground on the horizon to the right of the steeple in the center of the photo.

These units provided the anchor around which the retreating First and Eleventh Corps formed. A significant amount of artillery retreated to and went into firing position on the hill. The First and Eleventh Corps artillery consisted of a total of ten batteries with fifty-four guns. Nine of these batteries, forty-eight guns, initially fought west and north of Gettysburg. Retreating back to Cemetery Hill, eight batteries with thirty-two surviving guns joined with Wiedrich's for a total of thirty-eight guns. Resupplied with ammunition and under the central control of the two artillery brigade commanders, Colonel Charles S. Wainwright and Major Thomas W. Osborn, these nine batteries were deployed on both sides of the Baltimore Pike and covered the avenues of approach from the north, northeast, and northwest. Their presence was a significant obstacle to capturing the hill. In addition, retreating Union brigades rallied and joined the artillery on Cemetery Hill.[38]

The power of massed artillery under central command had been dramatically demonstrated earlier in the war. Exactly one year earlier to the day, at Malvern Hill eight batteries had been initially deployed along the Union defensive position. These guns had overwhelmed Lee's artillery and caused significant casualties among his attacking infantry, an infantry force much larger than that available to Ewell. At Stones River on January 2, 1863, fifty-seven of the Army of the Cumberland's guns were massed under the command of Captain John Mendenhall at McFadden's Ford and played a significant role in defeating an attack by a Confederate division.[39]

As much as Ewell may have wanted to conduct an attack to capture Cemetery Hill, the sorting out of all of the information on his mission, the friendly situation, and enemy forces must have given him pause. Even though there was a small window of opportunity when an attack might have captured Cemetery Hill, a force of two brigades was probably not strong enough to do it. For such an attack to have a chance of success, it would have required more combat power than was immediately available. The strength would be there with the arrival of Johnson's Division, but by then time had passed and the window of opportunity closed.

Interestingly, that night Lee issued an order for Ewell's Corps to move from its location north of Gettysburg back to the west and go into position next to Hill's Corps along Seminary Ridge. Ewell replied to Lee that he thought Culp's Hill was unoccupied and could be easily occupied the next day by part of his corps. Lee then rescinded his order, and Ewell's Corps remained in position, forming a right angle to the rest of the army as it deployed the next day.[40]

Had Ewell attacked Cemetery Hill, one of two outcomes might have occurred. First, if the attack was successful, then Meade's army would have been denied the key terrain on which it established its position at Gettysburg.

A different position would have had to be established farther south. Perhaps it would have been the Battle of Emmitsburg or Pipe Creek that went into the history books. Control of Cemetery Hill by Lee would have also given him control of the roads going south and southeast out of Gettysburg. These roads would have facilitated the movement of his concentrated army toward the Army of the Potomac and terrain objectives farther south.

Second, if Ewell's attack proved unsuccessful, the continued deployment of his corps north of Cemetery Hill may have been abandoned, and Lee might have enforced his instructions for the corps to redeploy to Seminary Ridge. With all three of his corps positioned on Seminary Ridge, Lee's ability to deliver a powerful attack on the Union south flank would have been greatly increased. Instead of two divisions marching south for the Union flank on July 2, there could have easily been four.

Neither of these events happened, and, when finally deployed, Lee's army formed a line north and west of Meade's position. This resulted in a Confederate position almost twice the length of the Union one, with the advantage of interior lines to Meade. As Wednesday changed into Thursday, the relative positions of the two armies had been fixed. These positions were a major factor in decisions made the following two days.

Meade Moves His Army to Gettysburg

Until Meade decided to move the remainder of the Army of the Potomac to Gettysburg there was no certainty that a major battle would be fought there.

George G. Meade had spent the prewar years in the U.S. Corps of Topographical Engineers. In August 1861 he was commissioned a brigadier general of volunteers. He commanded a brigade of infantry during the Seven Days and was wounded at Glendale. He returned to his brigade for Second Bull Run. Promoted to major general, he commanded a division during the 1862 Maryland Campaign and at Fredericksburg. At Chancellorsville he commanded the Fifth Corps. In the early morning hours of June 28, 1863, he was informed that he was the new commander of the Army of the Potomac.[41]

On the day he took command, the army was spread out in an uneven twenty-five-mile circle around Frederick, Maryland. Meade spent much of June 28 discovering the locations of his army and determining a course of action. Enclosed with the order naming him army commander was a letter from Major General Henry Halleck, the general in chief in Washington, providing overall mission guidance. Halleck's primary mission for Meade was to maintain the army between Lee and the capital. If Lee was to turn toward Baltimore or Washington, Halleck expected Meade to intercept the Confederate army before it reached either city. With this general guidance Meade formulated a campaign plan that moved his army in a north and northeast direction on a wide front. Orders were issued for the army to march the next day to Emmitsburg, Uniontown, Taneytown, Liberty, and New Windsor. On that same day, Lee, who had just issued the order for his army to concentrate, had two corps in the vicinity of Chambersburg and one corps at Carlisle with a division at York.[42]

Major General George G. Meade. National Archives.

On the morning of June 29, Meade placed his army in motion toward Harrisburg and at the same time covered the roads that led south to Baltimore and Washington. Meade's initial moves were designed to place his army between Lee and Baltimore or to engage him somewhere near Harrisburg, depending on Lee's movements. As Meade's army moved northward, he planned for its left flank to pass by or through Gettysburg. On June 30, Meade received sufficient information that indicated a large part of Lee's army was withdrawing from the vicinity of Carlisle and was concentrating at or east of Chambersburg. Meade thought Lee might use Cashtown Pass in South Mountain as a defensive position or as an avenue of approach to attack or maneuver around his army's left flank.[43]

By nightfall on June 30 both armies had moved closer to each other. Lee's concentration was well underway. Most of Hill's Corps had moved east through Cashtown Gap with an advance division at Cashtown. Longstreet's Corps was just behind Hill's. Two divisions of Ewell's Corps, marching from their forward positions, had reached Heidlersburg. The third division was in the Cumberland Valley and in position to march east and rejoin its corps. It appeared that Lee's order to concentrate the army before battle would be completed by nightfall the next day, July 1. On June 30 Meade's army had continued advancing north and northeast. At the end of the day, it

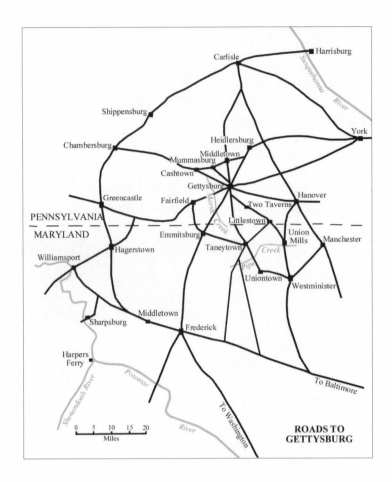

occupied positions along a line from the vicinity of Emmitsburg east to Littlestown, then southeast to Union Mills and Manchester. Cavalry was positioned to the left and right front of the army and had been actively engaged in obtaining intelligence.[44]

Meade's intent in marching north and northeast had been to protect Harrisburg from the threat of attack either by engaging or maneuvering Lee's army away from the Pennsylvania capital. As Meade began receiving information that Lee's advanced units were withdrawing from the Susquehanna River, he began to consider other options available to him.[45]

Meade knew that he could not allow Lee's army to move freely around the Pennsylvania countryside and that he must bring the armies into contact, and into battle. When the two armies were joined in battle, it was Meade's intent that it would be on terrain of his choosing and not Lee's.

Meade was also concerned that part of Lee's army was in the vicinity of Fairfield. If this was correct, then Lee might be maneuvering to attack his left flank or to take a position in the rear of his army. To guard against these possible threats and to have the options to defend or continue to advance, Meade ordered a reconnaissance made of favorable defensive terrain just south of Taneytown, Maryland, along Pipe Creek. This position was located about twenty miles southeast of Gettysburg along ground that would provide a tactical advantage for defensive operations. Meade issued a circular that assigned routes of withdrawal and locations for each corps along this position. This plan, if executed, envisioned the army moving from its present spread-out locations to a consolidated position, where it would assume a defensive posture against a southward Confederate move. It would provide Meade the advantages of fighting on ground of his choosing with the concentrated firepower of a defender. The circular was supposed to be issued on June 30, but a delay with the staff procedures prevented it from reaching corps commanders until the next day (and it is doubtful if Reynolds ever saw it), when it was surpassed by events.[46]

Some have pointed to this circular to show that Meade had made up his mind to retreat to defensive positions as soon as contact was made with Lee's army. A close reading of this document will show that it was in fact a contingency plan. Such plans are created to provide a course of action if specific conditions occur. Meade's plan had several conditional phrases, such as "If the enemy assumes the offense and attack" and "In the event these movements being necessary." Meade also did not limit himself to defense, and there is the sentence "Developments may cause the commanding general to assume the offense from his present positions." His actions echoing this last phrase, Meade issued orders for his army to continue moving north on July 1. The First and Eleventh Corps were ordered to Gettysburg. The Third Corps was ordered to move to Emmitsburg, thirteen miles from Gettysburg. The Fifth and Twelfth Corps were ordered to Hanover and Two Taverns, fifteen and eight miles from Gettysburg. The order also directed the Second Corps to Taneytown and the Sixth Corps to Manchester, fourteen and thirty-five miles, respectively, from Gettysburg. Meade's army was closer to Pipe Creek on June 30 than it would be after marching to the designated locations for July 1. Once Meade's corps reached these destinations, they would be, except for one corps, at least fifteen miles and in some cases more than twenty-five miles from Pipe Creek. These are not the dispositions Meade would have ordered if he had already made up his mind where to engage Lee.[47]

By the morning of July 1, Meade was prepared to move his army to the anticipated point of contact with the Confederate army near Gettysburg or to consolidate southeast of Gettysburg along Pipe Creek, in a previously reconnoitered defensive position. That morning saw Meade's units beginning the final moves that would commit the army to a major battle. Before noon Meade received reports that Buford and then Reynolds had engaged elements of Lee's army at Gettysburg. This was followed by information that Reynolds had ordered the army's left wing—the First, Eleventh, and Third Corps—to reinforce Buford. Soon after this he was informed of Reynolds's death. Meade then sent Major General Winfield S. Hancock, the Second Corps' commander, to Gettysburg. Hancock was ordered to assume overall tactical command and report as to the advisability of committing the army to a major battle at that location. Hancock arrived at Gettysburg around 4:00 P.M. and was instrumental in establishing the defensive positions on Cemetery Hill and Culp's Hill as the First and Eleventh Corps retreated back through the town and onto those key terrain features. He then sent his aide, Major Mitchell, to Meade with a verbal report and followed this with a written report. Hancock's reports informed Meade of the situation, and he advised that they could either retire (maybe back to Pipe Creek or Emmitsburg) or fight where they were, as the ground was favorable and a strong position could be developed. In the late afternoon orders were issued to the remaining corps to march to Gettysburg. Meade had committed his army to a major battle there.[48]

Meade's decision was the final step in a series of decisions that brought both armies to battle at Gettysburg. In the last days of June, he had received information that indicated where most of Lee's army was. On the morning of July 1 Meade was faced with three courses of action. First, he could continue to move his army north, looking to bring Lee into battle somewhere around Cashtown or Gettysburg. By moving forward, Meade could continue to close on Lee and engage him in battle. If he ceased movement or fell back, he might lose contact with the Confederate army. Second, Meade already had a contingency plan (the Pipe Creek circular) for defense on terrain of his choosing. Adoption of this course would surrender most of the tactical initiative to Lee. There was no guarantee that Lee would come to Pipe Creek, and the farther away Meade's army moved from Pipe Creek, the more difficult it would be to move back to it. Third, he could take up defensive positions on favorable terrain in the vicinity of Emmitsburg. Again this would surrender much of the tactical initiative to Lee, and there was no certainty Lee would march to Emmitsburg.

As the fighting developed on July 1 and as more of his corps continued to move north, Meade's options began to dwindle. Had he decided to execute his contingency plan for a defense along Pipe Creek, it is difficult to predict what might have happened. A withdrawal by that part of the Union Army, already engaged, may have been seen as a greater defeat than what occurred on July 1. Close pursuit by Lee might have prevented the corps that had been engaged on Wednesday from establishing their part of the defensive line along Pipe Creek. Lee might not have moved directly after Meade's army, but instead may have, after gathering his army together, maneuvered to turn Meade out of position and brought about a battle at a different location. The same scenario on a smaller scale applies to establishing a defense at Emmitsburg.

However, this is all speculation as Meade rose to the occasion and made the decision that provided his army with tactical direction, a clear mission, and a commitment to a major battle. Meade distinctly expressed his choice in a message to Halleck early in the evening of July 1, when he wrote, "I see no other course than to hazard a general battle."[49]

CHAPTER 3

THURSDAY, JULY 2, 1863

The fighting on July 1 was over by late afternoon and the limited window of opportunity to attack Cemetery Hill closed, but units continued to march toward Gettysburg and move into position. Before sunset, which was at 7:41 P.M., Rodes's Division and Early's Division took up positions in and to the east of Gettysburg. Half an hour later, as twilight turned to darkness, Johnson's Division arrived and formed the east-most part of Ewell's line. These three divisions formed the east-west segment of the Confederate position. In Hill's Corps, Pender's Division began the north-south portion of the position. Pender positioned his brigades from the Hagerstown (Fairfield) Road south along Seminary Ridge. This placed Pender's and Rodes's Divisions at a right angle with each other. The other two divisions of Hill's Corps remained behind Pender. The next morning these two divisions moved forward. Heth's Division went into a reserve position behind Pender's. Anderson's Division angled to the southeast, went into position on Pender's right, and extended the Confederate line south along Seminary Ridge. Farther west, two of Longstreet's divisions commenced moving toward Gettysburg on the Chambersburg Pike.[1]

The Army of the Potomac was also in motion. Before dark on Wednesday, the Twelfth Corps and part of the Third Corps joined the First and Eleventh Corps at Gettysburg. Early the next morning the remainder of the Third Corps, the Second and Fifth Corps, and the Artillery Reserve arrived. By mid-morning Meade's position was formed into the famous fishhook. Meade's last corps, the Sixth, arrived in the late afternoon.[2]

Lee Decides to Continue the Offense and Attack the Union Left

On July 2 Lee was confronted with the problem facing any commander who had just fought a surprise meeting engagement. Basically he had three options: attack, defend, or break contact (move away) and resume battle at a different location. Lee did not believe he could afford to remain in a defensive position east of South Mountain, waiting for the Army of the Potomac to attack him. His reasoning went to the availability of subsistence for his army and his concern for the security of the few mountain passes that led back into the Cumberland Valley. Lieutenant General James Longstreet offered Lee another course of action, which was a combination of two options: move away from the Union Army and reposition for defense at a different location, which would force Meade to attack.[3]

Graduating from West Point in 1842, Longstreet served in the Mexican War and on the western frontier before resigning in June 1861 and receiving an appointment as a brigadier general in the Confederate Army. In October 1861 he was promoted to major general and in October 1862 to lieutenant general. Except for Chancellorsville, he had participated in every major battle of the Army of Northern Virginia.[4]

Lieutenant General James Longstreet. National Archives.

Longstreet's experiences, especially at Fredericksburg, led him to the conclusion that the tactical defense had advantages over the tactical offense. He had personally seen how the increased range and accuracy of the rifled musket and cannon, especially when protected by a fold in the ground, a sunken road, a wall, or breastworks, gave the defenders a decided advantage.[5]

An attacking infantry force coming into view at a thousand yards required approximately thirteen to sixteen minutes to close to hand-to-hand range with the defending force. In rough terrain the attacker would move slower and increase the exposure time. Marching at quick-time, it would take the attacker twelve to fifteen minutes to move from one thousand to one hundred yards from the defenders. The last one hundred yards would be crossed in one minute as the attacker went to double quick-time. The exposure time would be increased if the attacking infantry stopped to fire at the defenders. During these thirteen to sixteen minutes of exposure, the attackers would constantly be under artillery fire from one thousand yards to the defender's position. In the last one hundred yards, they would be under fire from the defending infantry. During this exposure time one cannon as a minimum could fire thirteen rounds and one infantryman three rounds. A defending infantry regiment of three hundred to four hundred soldiers would fire nine hundred to twelve hundred rounds and an artillery battery fifty-two (four-gun battery) to seventy-eight (six-gun battery) rounds. Multiply these by two, three, or four regiments and/or batteries, and you begin to gain an appreciation of the volume of fire delivered against attacking infantry as they closed with the defenders.

As the second ranking officer in the Army of Northern Virginia, Longstreet had a duty to offer advice and counsel to Lee. Longstreet recommended that Lee move the army south of Gettysburg and take up a position across the roads to Washington and Baltimore. Such a move by Lee could have presented Meade with the threat to his left flank and rear that had earlier concerned him. Longstreet believed this would force Meade to attack while the Southern forces had the advantage of a strong defensive position. This concept of strategic offense and tactical defense would still have allowed Lee to maintain the operational initiative.[6]

There are four types of offensive operations: movement to contact, attack, exploitation, and pursuit. A movement to contact is conducted by a force when the commander is unsure of the exact enemy location and force. An attack, which uses various forms of maneuver, is conducted to destroy or render combat-ineffective an enemy force or to capture key terrain. Exploitation often follows a successful attack with the purpose of preventing the enemy from reestablishing the defense and to capture objectives deep in the enemy's rear area. A pursuit, like the exploitation, follows a successful attack and can also follow a successful exploitation. While the exploitation orients on capture of terrain, the pursuit orients on the enemy force. The purpose of the pursuit is to cut off, capture, or destroy an enemy force that is attempting to escape. Lee's army had been conducting a movement to contact on July 1. The next day Lee decided to continue on the offense and attacked. If his attack had been successful, Lee could have transitioned to the pursuit or exploitation.[7]

There are five forms of maneuver that can be used when conducting an attack: envelopment, turning movement, infiltration, penetration, and frontal attack. The envelopment avoids the enemy front and maneuvers against one or both flanks. The single envelopment is against one flank, and the double envelopment is against both flanks. Some authors refer to these as flank attacks. The purpose of the envelopment is to collapse the defender's flank, gain the enemy rear area to isolate him, and control his lines of communication. An attacking force uses a turning movement to avoid the enemy's principal defensive position by seizing objectives in the enemy rear and causing him to move out of his current position or divert major forces against a new threat. The presence of a force in the enemy's rear turns him out of his position. The infiltration is a form of maneuver in which an attacking force moves undetected through or into an area occupied by the enemy to a position of advantage in the enemy rear. The penetration is used to cause a break in the enemy's defensive position. This maneuver will create assailable flanks at the point of penetration and provide access to enemy rear areas. A frontal attack strikes the enemy across a wide front and over the most direct approaches. Success with this form of maneuver depends on achieving an advantage in combat power throughout the attack. It can be the most costly form of maneuver.[8]

Longstreet's recommended course of action was for Lee to conduct a turning movement, then temporarily go on the defense and force Meade to attack them on ground of their choosing.

Lee, on the other hand, did not believe the turning movement advocated by Longstreet was a viable course of action. His army was already facing a large part of Meade's, and the area to the south of Gettysburg was not familiar ground to the Confederates. If the army was to move south and occupy a favorable position between Meade and Washington, exactly where was this position, what roads would take them there, and how would the left flank be protected during the march? To develop such a plan, answers to those questions had to be found. The best organization to do this was the cavalry, which unfortunately was off on a raid or spread out in the Cumberland Valley. With no capability of obtaining the information he required, Lee could not even consider moving his army to the south. This left Lee with the options of penetration, frontal attack, or envelopment. Lee believed he had insufficient force to conduct a penetration or a frontal attack. Thus he selected the option of an envelopment. This course of action presented the possibility of bringing concentrated combat power against a weaker defender at the point of contact; it allowed him to keep the initiative, forcing Meade to respond to him; and it supported one of Lee's major objectives of defeating the Army of the Potomac on Northern soil.[9]

Lee initially thought that he might make his main attack against the Union right, using Ewell's Corps and other supporting units. However, after talking to Ewell and his division commanders, he decided to make his main attack on the Union left flank. As Lee looked east from Seminary Ridge on the morning of July 2, he was faced with a series of problems that had to be solved if his attack was going to be successful. These problems centered on the Union defenses, the terrain occupied by the two armies, and the time available.[10]

The Army of the Potomac occupied a position that went from Culp's Hill west to Cemetery Hill and then south along Cemetery Ridge to the vicinity of Little Round Top. This line was about three miles in length and has been described as resembling a fishhook with the barb at Culp's Hill, the shank along Cemetery Ridge, and the eye of the shank at the Round Tops. The curve in the Union line resulted in the right and left flanks of Meade's army being only two miles apart across the line of a semicircle. This gave Meade the advantage of interior lines with the capability to shift forces from one flank to another in a shorter period of time than Lee could. Lee's position, on the other hand, was the more extended one. His position began east of Gettysburg. From there it went one and one-half miles west through the town to Seminary Ridge. There it turned south and went along Seminary Ridge for about two miles and later an additional one and one-fourth miles. Lee's position was almost five miles in length and was generally shaped as a right angle with the Union army on the inside of the angle. This resulted in Lee not being able to move forces on the direct line between his two flanks. Any units moved by him must go along the longer outside route. The longer distance also made coordination of action between opposite flank units difficult.

As Lee looked east from Seminary Ridge, he must have realized that the ground favored Meade. The ground between Seminary Ridge and Cemetery Ridge was open and rolling, with long fields of fire and observation. He could easily see the north anchor of the Union line— Cemetery Hill— and visualize Culp's Hill to its east. From there, as he looked from his left to his right, he could see the long feature of Cemetery Ridge as it descended from Cemetery Hill to the low ground farther south. Looking away to his right front, his gaze would have fallen on what would become the south anchor of Meade's position—the Round Tops. This casual observation would reveal that no position on Seminary Ridge, except for the southern part of Cemetery Ridge, was higher than any observable location on the Union line. Lee realized that, with the Union advantage of higher position and its longer observation, the lateral movement of his attack force must be behind the cover of tree lines or along low ground to the rear of his position. Failure to keep his envelopment concealed, as it moved into position, would reveal his intentions to Meade, providing him the opportunity to reposition forces to meet the threat.

The center of Meade's position on Cemetery Ridge as Lee might have seen it on July 2.

The left of Meade's position as Lee might have seen it on July 2. Little Round Top and Big Round Top are in the right center of the photo.

In an attempt to overcome these two Union advantages, Lee devised an attack plan to send Longstreet with two divisions and his artillery on a march through low ground behind Seminary Ridge to a position on the south flank of Meade's line. Earlier that morning Captain Samuel R. Johnston of Lee's staff had led a small group on a reconnaissance to the south. He reported to Lee that there were no Union troops in the vicinity of Big Round Top or Little Round Top. However, this information was incorrect. Based on Johnston's report and what he could observe, Lee believed the southern portion of the Union line was "upon the high ground along the Emmitsburg road, with a steep ridge in rear, which was also occupied." When Longstreet reached the Peach Orchard, he was to face northeast and assault Meade's left flank by attacking parallel to the Emmitsburg Road toward Cemetery Hill. As he began his attack, Anderson's Division of Hill's Corps would join in and attack the Union center. At the same time Longstreet began his attack, Ewell, to keep Union brigades in position, was to conduct a demonstration against Culp's Hill and Cemetery Hill, with the discretion to turn it into an attack.[11]

Attacks against an enemy position are categorized as main and supporting attacks. The main attack is the one the commander has designed to capture the enemy's position or key terrain to achieve his overall objective. Usually it has the majority of troops assigned to it and has priority of supporting artillery fire. The reserve is normally placed so as to be able to support or exploit the success of the main attack. Supporting attacks are designed to assist the main attack by causing the enemy to disperse his forces and fight in several locations, to pin enemy forces in position, to cause a premature and incorrect commitment of enemy reserves, and to confuse the enemy as to which is the main attack. So it was with Lee's plan. Longstreet's two divisions were the main attack, with Ewell and Hill providing forces for

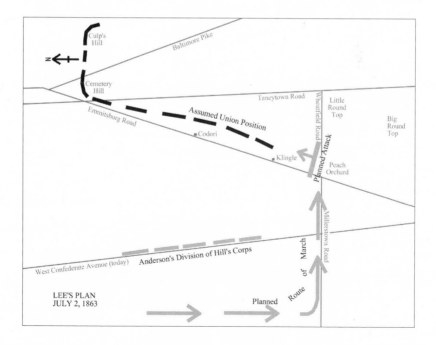

the supporting attack. The disadvantages of Lee's plan were no reserve to support the main attack or to exploit success, no army-level artillery reserve with which to add weight to the main attack, and no practical coordination between Longstreet's and Ewell's attacks because of the distance between them. The advantages that Lee might have expected would be the element of surprise if Longstreet's divisions could move to their attack positions without being seen, the relative strength at the point of contact, and the chance to hold potential Union reinforcements in position with the supporting attacks.

Time was the other problem facing Lee, and time did not favor him. Civil War armies normally did not conduct night attacks. It was difficult to control long battle lines in the smoke of gunfire and in woods; it was impossible in the dark. Lee issued his order to Longstreet sometime around 10:00 A.M., and Longstreet began the march south about noon. The distance from where the lead brigade of the column started marching to its designated attack position was 3.3 miles. Average speed of a marching column was 2.25 to 2.5 miles per hour. At that speed, if all went well, Lee could reasonably expect the lead elements to move into attack positions around 1:30 P.M. Longstreet's column was composed of two divisions, four battalions of artillery, and a combat supply train of perhaps 150 wagons. This formation had a road space of just under eight miles and at a normal march speed required 3.5 hours to pass a given point. With units deploying simultaneously, this time could be cut down to about 1.5 to 2 hours. At best, therefore, by the time the infantry and artillery were deployed for attack, it would be about 3:00 or 3:30 P.M. Sunset was 7:41 P.M., and by 8:13 P.M. it would be too dark to conduct an attack. If the attack began at 3:00 P.M., there would be five hours of daylight to complete it.[12]

By late morning on July 2, Lee had considered his options and decided on an aggressive course of action. His plan was designed to minimize any advantages Meade had because of his position. Lee, as a result of his decision, gave up the opportunity to change the location of the battle by moving to a different area or to redeploy his army into a more compact position by moving Ewell's Corps back to Seminary Ridge. Lee's decision maintained the initiative for his army and kept Meade on the defense. However, the attack was conducted prior to the arrival of Longstreet's last division, Pickett's, and this reduced the potential strength of the main attack by almost one-third. Lee's decision, to continue on the offense and to attack on the south flank, set the course of the battle for that day and the following one.

Longstreet Orders the Countermarch

Time was a critical factor in Lee's planning for July 2 as it favored the defender, not the attacker. Early in the morning additional units of Meade's army arrived, and in the afternoon his last corps, the Sixth, rejoined the army. As for Lee, with the late-morning arrival of the last brigade of Longstreet's Corps to reach the battlefield that day, he had received all of his force that would be available for action on the second day.

Longstreet received his orders, gathered up the last brigade of his two divisions, and at noon was marching south. The march commenced with McLaws's Division leading and Hood's Division following. Brigadier General Joseph Kershaw's brigade was the lead unit of McLaws's Division. To reach a position on the Union flank required a march of just over three miles for Kershaw's Brigade and somewhat farther for the rest of the force. Kershaw's Brigade began its march from just north of Black Horse Tavern, crossed the Hagerstown (Fairfield) Road, and continued on south. In one-half mile the road came to the crest of a small ridge. At this location the flags of a Union signal station on Little Round Top were visible.[13]

Signal stations had a dual role. They provided communication between the army's senior commanders and functioned as part of a relay to pass

The high ground on Black Horse Tavern Road, where Longstreet realized that his column would be seen by the Union signal station on Little Round Top if it continued on. Big Round Top is on the horizon in the center of the photo. To the left of Big Round Top is Little Round Top, which cannot be seen today because of the trees on Seminary Ridge.

messages along a line of communication. In this case the signal relay went from Meade's headquarters south to Frederick, Maryland, and then by telegraph to Washington. A second role was intelligence gathering. The signalmen were located on high ground with good long-range observation potential, and they had binoculars and telescopes to aid observation, as well as the means to communicate what they saw. The signal station on Little Round Top had a direct line of sight to Meade's headquarters. From their position on Little Round Top, the signal troops could observe the area of the ridge that Longstreet's force would have to cross if it continued along the Black Horse Tavern Road.

McLaws, riding ahead of his division, immediately stopped the march when he saw the signal station on Little Round Top. When the column halted, Longstreet rode up to McLaws to find out what the problem was. On reaching the crest of the ridge, he realized that, if McLaws's Division continued forward, it would be seen and lose the element of surprise in Lee's planned envelopment. Once McLaws's men were observed, Meade, depending on the speed of communication, might reposition additional forces on his south flank before Longstreet began his attack. A quick look around the area did not come up with an alternate route. Longstreet then decided that they must turn around and go back to near where they started and move by a different route.[14]

By this time the lead brigades of Hood's Division and the rear brigades of McLaws's Division were crowded side by side on Black Horse Tavern Road. This happened because McLaws's Division had moved down a country lane that led it into the road, while Hood's division had marched along the road. When Hood's Division reached the intersection with the lane, it did not stop and wait until all of McLaws's Division had passed by and then follow behind. Hood's brigades continued to march along the road, and now there were overlapping march columns. These crowded conditions immediately became worse when McLaws turned the head of his division around and proceeded to retrace its steps. A simple move of reversing direction became a time-consuming traffic jam. Taking too much time, McLaws was nevertheless able to reach the vicinity of the initial starting point, where he found a new route. With Kershaw's Brigade leading, McLaws's and Hood's Divisions stayed out of observation from the Union position and moved south along the course of Willoughby Run. After rejoining Black Horse Tavern Road, they continued on to Pitzer's School House. There they turned left (east) and marched along Millerstown Road, which they thought would place their divisions on the Union left flank. The countermarch added three miles and one hour and twenty minutes to the march for the lead units and from one to two more miles for the remainder. This additional time brought the lead brigades to their attack positions around 3:00 P.M. rather than 1:30.[15]

It is interesting to note that earlier in the day Colonel E. Porter Alexander had been ordered to move his artillery battalion to the same location that the infantry was trying to reach. When he encountered the same ridgeline along the route of march, Alexander turned to the right. To avoid being seen from Little Round Top, the artillery kept below the crest of the ridge, moved west for a short distance, then south and east to Pitzer's School House, and finally east along the road, where they stopped to wait for the infantry. Colonel Alexander then retraced his route back to where he found the infantry stopped while a decision was being made as to what to do next. He pointed out to one of Longstreet's staff officers (probably Moxley Sorrel) the route he had taken, but he was told not to approach Longstreet because of the general's bad mood. Alexander then left and returned to the artillery.[16]

Marching east along the Millerstown Road, McLaws expected to cross over the southern end of Seminary Ridge and continue on for 700 yards (0.4 miles), where his division would cross the Emmitsburg Road. From there it was to continue east through the Peach Orchard and along the Wheatfield

At the Peach Orchard looking north towards Cemetery Hill (center of photo). Lee's plan called for McLaws's Division to attack from this location across the open ground to what he incorrectly presumed to be the position of Meade's left flank.

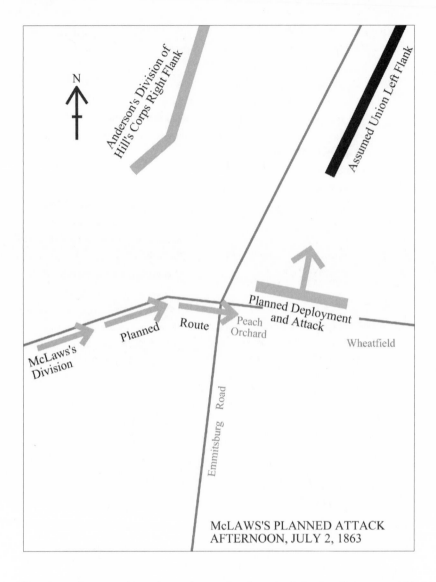

McLAWS'S PLANNED ATTACK
AFTERNOON, JULY 2, 1863

Road just far enough so that, when it faced to the left, the division would be facing northeast with its left flank next to the Emmitsburg Road. This maneuver was to position McLaws's Division on the left flank of the Union line, which was believed to be about one-half mile north of the Peach Orchard and generally along or east of the Emmitsburg Road. Of course, the left flank of the Union main line had never been in this position. But what Kershaw discovered as his brigade came to the crest of the ridge surprised everyone.[17]

Directly to Kershaw's front, in the Peach Orchard and to the north and southeast of the orchard, were Union infantry and artillery. With the later-than-anticipated arrival at the southern part of Seminary Ridge, more time was consumed while Lee's plan was modified to take into account the situation that was presented to Longstreet and McLaws.[18]

The problems encountered during Longstreet's Corps' march to its attack positions were caused by the lack of good information on the roads, the terrain, especially where Black Horse Tavern Road was exposed to observation from Little Round Top, incorrect assumptions about where the left flank of the Union defensive position was, and no information or indication that Major General Daniel E. Sickles's Third Corps occupied positions along the Emmitsburg Road and at the Peach Orchard.

Many of these problems could have been reduced or eliminated by effective staff work at the army and corps level. A knowledge of the roads and some form of traffic control by the staff officers could have assured a logical sequencing of divisions on to Black Horse Tavern Road and prevented the overlapping columns.

Although Lee had sent out reconnaissance parties from his staff, the primary organization for acquiring information on road networks, terrain, obstacles, and enemy positions was the cavalry, of which Lee had none readily available. Had any sizable force of cavalry been available, it could have performed a reconnaissance of Longstreet's intended route of march and kept the proposed attack positions under observation. This probably would have prevented the countermarch and kept Longstreet and his commanders from being surprised by the unexpected forward Third Corps position. It could have provided time for a revised plan to be developed prior to contact between the opposing forces. It is even possible that early correct and timely information might have prevented Lee from developing a flawed plan that was based on an incorrect assumption as to where the Union left flank was. Again, Fitz-Hugh Lee's cavalry brigade at Chancellorsville on May 2, 1863, presents an example of what might have happened at Gettysburg on the second day had cavalry been present.

Through incomplete reconnaissance at all levels of command and failure of coordination and communication, a decision was made that turned what could have been a relatively simple march to an attack position into a complicated and time-consuming series of moves and countermoves. Longstreet's decision pushed the time of attack to very late in the afternoon, disrupted the coordination and readiness of both wings of Lee's army to work with each other more closely, and provided additional time for Meade's last corps, the Sixth, to arrive on the battlefield.

Sickles Moves Forward to the Peach Orchard

As the leading units of McLaws's Division came up on the crest of the southern end of Seminary Ridge, they were surprised to find their forward progress blocked by a Union battle line. This line was part of Major General Daniel E. Sickles's Third Corps, which was located three-fourths of a mile farther west of where it had been positioned earlier in the day.

The Third Corps was composed of two divisions, each with three brigades, and an artillery brigade with five batteries. Part of the corps had arrived just before dark on July 1 and the remainder the morning of the following day. Sickles's initial position was to the left of the Second Corps with his right touching the Second Corps' left in the vicinity of the George Weikert farmhouse on the southern end of Cemetery Ridge. From there the Third Corps line ran south for 1,300 yards (0.7 miles) to Little Round Top. While both of his flanks were on good defensible terrain, the center of Sickles's line was located in less desirable low ground that paralleled Plum Run.[19]

Fourteen hundred yards west of Sickles's initial position, the Emmitsburg Road passes over a small plateau. This plateau is thirty to forty feet higher in elevation than the center of Sickles's line. In the area of the Peach Orchard, this plateau has depth as well as width, which made it an ideal position for Civil War artillery. As it is higher than the ground along Plum Run, occupation by Confederate forces would provide two significant tactical advantages. First, sufficient Confederate artillery in position there might gain fire superiority and dominate a large segment of the Third Corps line. Second, from that location artillery could provide supporting fire for infantry attacks not only in an easterly direction but also to the northeast. When Sickles looked west from the center of his initial position, these advantages must have been very evident to him.[20]

Forty-three years old at Gettysburg, Sickles was a professional politician who had been a New York state senator and then a U.S. congressman. He received notoriety when he killed his wife's lover, Barton Key—son of Francis Scott key, the author of the "Star Spangled Banner"—and was acquitted. Commissioned a brigadier general in 1861 and promoted to major general in November 1862, he fought on the Peninsula, at Fredericksburg, and at Chancellorsville. During the Battle of Chancellorsville, Sickles had been ordered to give up a position at Hazel Grove. This position was on elevated key terrain that provided Sickles's infantry and artillery a significant tactical advantage. The abandonment of the Hazel Grove position relinquished the advantage to the Confederates, especially the artillery, and was a key position in Lee's successful attack on May 3, 1863. As he observed the ground to his front on July 2, the memory of Hazel Grove, just two months before, must have been foremost in his mind.[21]

Meade ordered Sickles to place his corps along Cemetery Ridge from the left of Hancock's Second Corps to Little Round Top. However, Sickles decided that he could not allow the piece of key terrain along the Emmitsburg Road to remain unoccupied and ordered his corps forward. When his line was reestablished, the right flank of his position was 1,000 yards north of the Peach Orchard. From that location it went southwest along the

Major General Daniel E. Sickles. Library of Congress.

Emmitsburg Road to the Peach Orchard. There it turned east and went 800 yards to the Wheatfield, where it then went south another 800 yards to Devil's Den. Devil's Den was the left flank of Sickles's position. There Sickles ran out of troops before he ran out of ground that needed to be occupied. As a result, neither Little Round Top, some 500 yards east of Devil's Den, nor Big Round Top, 650 yards to the southeast, was occupied by a significant Union force.[22]

While we might agree with Sickles's analysis of the terrain to his front and his desire to deny an excellent position to Confederate artillery, one has to fault his execution. No timely or aggressive attempt was made by him to inform General Meade of his intention to move forward. At the time that Sickles moved forward to the Emmitsburg Road and the Peach Orchard, Meade's reserve was Major General George Sykes's Fifth Corps. Sykes's corps, composed of three infantry divisions and an artillery brigade of five batteries, was concentrated along the Baltimore Pike in the vicinity of Rock Creek. Had Meade been aware, in a timely fashion, of Sickles's redeployment forward, he could have easily moved all or part of the Fifth Corps in an orderly fashion from its reserve position to occupy Little Round Top, to fill in the gaps in the line, or to support Sickles's position. He had to attempt to do it anyway in the confusion of the fighting that followed.[23]

Sickles's move forward set the character of the fighting on the south flank. When Longstreet's Corps arrived on the southern part of Seminary Ridge, he expected to find the Union flank to his left, somewhere along or east of the Emmitsburg Road. This part of Lee's plan was flawed, as the Union flank was never where he assumed it to be. Had Sickles not moved forward, Longstreet could have continued to move forward, deploying McLaws's Division as it reached the area of the Rose Farm and the Wheat-field. Hood's Division might have been deployed to the right of McLaws's or ordered to follow in a supporting role, thereby adding depth to the attack. Deploying to the right would have resulted in Hood advancing through Devil's Den, then making contact with the left of the Sickles's line as he approached Little Round Top. The result of this deployment would have been a more compact battle line for the Confederates. It would have also given Longstreet the possibility of flanking Little Round Top on the south as his attack moved east and northeast. Another option would have been for Hood's Division to deploy behind McLaws's Division, using it to protect his flank, and with Major General Richard H. Anderson's division joining in the attack, advance northeast (as Lee had initially intended) and strike the Union position. This option could have exposed Longstreet to a counter-attack by the Third or Fifth Corps.

However, this was not what Longstreet found. Instead he encountered in front of him a Union force whose position went off to his right. Faced with this situation, he was forced into the time-consuming activity of de-ploying one division, while at the same time trying to find the Union flank, moving his other division to the right, and deploying it into a battle line. These actions consumed more of the remaining time available for the attack and established the parameters for the fighting on the south flank.

Longstreet Attacks the Union Left

It was approximately 3:00 P.M. or a little later when McLaws's Division marched the last few hundred yards up the western side of Seminary Ridge. Longstreet rode up to McLaws and inquired, "How are you going in?" Ac-cording to McLaws, he replied, "That will be determined when I can see what is in my front." To this Longstreet said, "There is nothing to your front; you will be entirely on the flank of the enemy." McLaws then stated, "Then I will continue my march in column of companies, and after arriving on the flank as far as necessary will face to the left and march on the enemy." This conversation was a reflection of Lee's assumption as to where the Union flank was when he issued orders for Longstreet's march and attack. How-

Sickles's position at the Peach Orchard as seen by the lead element of Longstreet's column as it came on South Seminary Ridge. The Peach Orchard is in the left of the photo; the Wheatfield is behind the trees in the center; and Little Round Top is to the right.

ever, as the Confederate commanders discovered when they reached the crest of the ridge, the situation, much to their surprise, was totally different from that envisioned by Lee and others. Not only was a Union force directly across their line of march, but the Union position extended south past the Confederate right.[24]

As Longstreet observed what he could see of Sickle's position, it was evident to him that Lee's initial plan was unworkable. However, he understood Lee's intention: to attack the flank of the Union army. Longstreet now began to position his force to comply with his commander's intent. McLaws's Division was deployed on either side of the road that went over the crest of Seminary Ridge. Kershaw's Brigade was placed on the right (south) side of the road while Brigadier General William Barksdale's brigade deployed on the left. Brigadier General Paul Semmes's brigade went in position behind Kershaw's, and Brigadier General William Wofford placed his brigade behind Barksdale's. Instead of the envelopment that Lee had envisioned, McLaws's Division was positioned for a frontal attack on the south end of the Union position. Hood was ordered to move his division to the right, under the protection of the ridge and woods, to a location near the Emmitsburg Road. When this move had been completed, Brigadier General Jerome Robertson's brigade was deployed astride the Emmitsburg

Road. To Robertson's right was Brigadier General Evander Law's brigade. Brigadier General George T. Anderson's brigade was in a supporting position behind Robertson, and Brigadier General Henry Benning's brigade was behind Law's. The battle line formed by these brigades faced generally northeast. Robertson and Law were positioned so that when they moved forward, Robertson would strike the flank of the Union line at Devil's Den, and Law, on his right, would move over Big Round Top and on to Little Round Top. At this time both of the Round Tops were unoccupied. By the time McLaws and Hood had deployed their divisions, it was about 4:00 P.M. Longstreet had indeed placed a force, even if late in the day, in position to carry out Lee's intent of striking the left flank of the Army of the Potomac.[25]

While Major General John B. Hood's Division was deploying into an attack formation, he sent out scouts to determine what was to his front. Hood had graduated from West Point in 1853 and served in California and Texas until April 1861, when he resigned his U.S. Army commission and entered Confederate service. Promoted to brigadier general in March 1862 and then major general in October 1862, he had served as a brigade commander at the Seven Days and a division commander at Second Bull Run, Antietam, and Fredericksburg. By the time of the Battle of Gettysburg, he had a reputation as one of the most, if not the most, aggressive commander in Lee's army.[26]

Hood's reconnaissance showed that Big Round Top was unoccupied, as was the ground to the east of the Round Tops. This information led Hood to recommend several times to Longstreet that his division should not attack from where it was positioned but should move to the right (east) and attack north, passing to the east side of the Round Tops. Essentially the axis of advance for Hood's proposed attack would have been north, astride the Taneytown Road, into the left rear of the Meade's army.[27]

When presented with this option, Longstreet, like any other commander on the scene, had to consider the pros and cons of again

Major General John B. Hood. Library of Congress.

changing the attack plan. Longstreet knew that the other attacking elements of Lee's army were keyed to his attack. Major General Richard H. Anderson's division of Hill's Third Corps was in position to the left of McLaws' Division and prepared to attack. Off to the northeast, on the left of the Confederate position, brigades of Ewell's Corps were also preparing to attack the Union positions on Culp's Hill and Cemetery Hill. However, none of these attacks would commence until Longstreet began the main attack. With the arrival of McLaws's Division in front of the Union defenses rather than on their flank, the element of surprise in Lee's plan was lost. The defenders were not only aware of McLaws's position, but also Hood's. Of the five artillery battalions in Longstreet's Corps, one had deployed directly in front of the Peach Orchard, and two had gone into positions farther south to support the attack. Most of this artillery was now firing on the Union positions, and in turn was being fired on by Union artillery located along the Emmitsburg Road, in the Peach Orchard, along Wheatfield Road, and in Devil's Den.[28]

Longstreet had to consider what would happen when Hood marched farther to the east. McLaws's Division was only seven hundred yards from the Union position in the Peach Orchard. Could McLaws remain as he was,

Little Round Top and Big Round Top as seen from the left of Hood's attack position. The argument between Hood and Longstreet about whether to attack or move farther to the right occurred where this photo was taken.

or would he have to thin out his line by extending it to the south and occupy part of the ground vacated by Hood? Would the Union troops to his front allow him to do this? Consideration had to be given as to how Hood would reach an attack position farther east. Then, as today, there was a road about seven-tenths of a mile behind Hood's location. This road intersected with the Emmitsburg Road and went east for 1.7 miles to the Taneytown Road. A march along this road would place his division where Hood wanted to be. We do not know the condition of the road in 1863, nor do we know if Hood had sent someone on a reconnaissance of the road, or even knew of its existence. Again there was the factor of time. It would have required at least two and one-half hours, maybe longer, for Hood's entire division to march farther to the east and then deploy. This would place them in position to attack no earlier than 6:30 P.M. but probably even later. Hood may have considered moving his division cross-country to a new attack position. This would have been a march of 1.7 miles, but it would have been through woods and over elevated terrain. The movement speed would have been reduced, and thus the time to reach an attack position on the Taneytown Road would have been about the same.

Once Hood had moved farther to the east, he would be separated from the rest of the army and unsupported. What of the Union forces in the area? Hood's troops had already been seen. If Hood's infantry was observed moving south or to the east, it would not be difficult to surmise what they were up to.

Shortly after the Confederate and Union artillery in the vicinity of the Peach Orchard and Emmitsburg Road began firing at each other, Meade ordered Sykes to move his Fifth Corps from the Baltimore Pike to the Union left. Two of Sykes's divisions had departed and marched toward the left. However, one division was still between the Baltimore Pike and the Taneytown Road. Also in this area was the artillery park of the reserve artillery. Many of the reserve batteries had been sent to different parts of the field, but there remained, depending on the time, some four to six batteries with twenty-four to thirty-four guns in the area between the Taneytown Road and the Baltimore Pike. Any part of or all of this infantry-artillery force could have been used to oppose Hood's recommended attack. In mid-afternoon one of Meade's largest corps, the Sixth, under command of Major General John Sedgwick, began arriving on the Baltimore Pike in the rear of the Union position. This three-division corps, with its six-battery artillery brigade, was a powerful force and positioned to deploy against any flank attack or penetration.[29]

The question of time had to be a major factor in weighing the options. The move into their current positions had taken Longstreet's two divisions longer than planned. More time would be required to redeploy Hood's Division farther east. This delay might have meant that there would not be enough time to conduct the attack that day. A postponement of the attack until the next day could mean the addition of Major General George Pickett's division. However, it would give Meade the night of July 2–3, and perhaps even the early morning hours of July 3, to withdraw Sickle's corps back to its initial defensive position, reposition additional forces to the left flank, and develop a compact and coordinated defensive position.

The loss of the element of surprise, the unexpected positions of Sickles's Third Corps, the loss of time in conducting the countermarch, the rapidly approaching night, and a lack of additional forces all contributed to limiting Longstreet's courses of action. He decided that his corps must attack from the positions now occupied by his two divisions. McLaws's Division attacked the Union positions centered on the Peach Orchard and the ground to the east. Hood's Division went for Devil's Den and Little Round Top.

Law Goes for the Artillery

This decision was an almost routine tactical decision that was being made by brigade commanders as they maneuvered and fought their brigades throughout the three days of the battle. However, this decision would define the scope and character of the battle on the extreme southern flank. It had major consequences, not only on the brigades involved, but also for their division, corps, and army.

Hood deployed his division for the attack with two brigades in the first line, Robertson's on the left and Law's on the right. Law's Brigade was not only the right-most unit of the division, it was the right-flank brigade of the corps and the army. Anderson's and Benning's Brigades formed the second or supporting line. Benning's task, as a part of the second line, was to follow and be prepared to support or reinforce Law's attack.[30]

Evander Law had fought in every major battle in the east—

Brigadier General Evander M. Law. Library of Congress.

first as a regimental commander, then as a brigade commander—from First Bull Run, where he was severely wounded, to Fredericksburg. His brigade was composed of five Alabama regiments, which he positioned in line from left to right: Fourth, Forty-seventh, Fifteenth, Forty-fourth, and Forty-eighth. Moving forward from their position should have brought them over and around Big Round Top and to the south and southeast slopes of Little Round Top.[31]

When Law's brigade moved forward, it received artillery fire from Captain James E. Smith's Fourth New York Battery, located on the rocky plateau above Devil's Den, which was to the brigade's left front. To stop

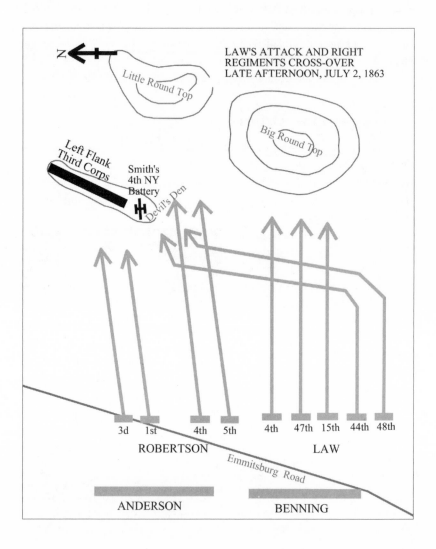

this fire, Law ordered his two right regiments—the Forty-fourth and Forty-eighth—to pull out of line, pass to the left behind the other three regiments, and attack Smith's battery. While carrying out this maneuver, these two regiments went too far to the left and reentered the battle line in the middle of Robertson's Brigade, which was on Law's left. The immediate consequence of this was the mixing of Robertson's and Law's Brigades, which brought on a breakdown of command and control and coordination. Part of Robertson's Brigade attacked Devil's Den with Law's two regiments, while the remainder of his brigade attacked Little Round Top. After the shifting of regiments, the two regiments, which had previously been in the left center and center of the line, were now the brigade's two right regiments. These two regiments, the Forty-seventh and Fifteenth Alabama, continued on over Big Round Top and attacked the Twentieth Maine, which was the extreme left regiment of the Union army.[32]

Had the Forty-fourth and Forty-eighth not been redeployed from their original position on the brigade's right, they may have outflanked the Union position on Little Round Top and found themselves on the Taneytown Road. Depending on the time in the afternoon, length of time for the threat to be communicated to Meade, and availability of reserves, the defenses on

Meade's left flank as seen from the right part of Hood's Division's attack position. Little Round Top is in the center of the photo, Big Round Top is to the right, and Devil's Den to the left. Law's Brigade attacked from the location where this photo was taken forward across the open field and into the woods.

Little Round Top might have been taken from the rear. The effect of Law's decision was compounded by another one.

Benning Follows the Wrong Attack

Henry L. Benning was a Georgia politician turned soldier. A colonel commanding a regiment at Second Bull Run, he was, by Fredericksburg, a brigade commander. His brigade was in the supporting second line about four hundred yards behind Law's. When the attack commenced, his brigade moved forward and through a line of woods. As Benning came out of the woods, he saw troops in front of him moving in an attack. He believed this was Law's entire brigade, which he decided to follow in a supporting role. What Benning saw were the two Alabama regiments from Law's right as they shifted left. When Benning followed these two regiments, he placed his brigade behind the attack moving on Devil's Den. There he added the weight of his brigade to the capture of Devil's Den.[33]

In the meantime, the regiments of Law's Brigade now on the right fought themselves to exhaustion in attacks against the left-flank Union regiments on Little Round Top. These two unsupported regiments had insufficient strength to break the Union left on Little Round Top. Had Benning

continued moving forward and not been drawn to the left by Law's two regiments, he would have eventually made contact with the majority of Law's brigade, which was attacking the defenses on Little Round Top. One can only conjecture as to further results. But the arrival of a fresh Confederate brigade against the Union position on the south side of Little Round Top could well have resulted in the loss of that key position and the collapse of the Union left.

Lee had planned for two divisions, eight brigades, to envelope Meade's left flank. Late in the afternoon his available

Brigadier General Henry L. Benning. Library of Congress.

The attack position of Hood's Division as seen from Little Round Top. That position was along the far wood line. The gap in the woods is where the Emmitsburg Road is located. The division's right half was positioned where the open ground can barely be seen in the left part of the photo.

forces for this were reduced to just two brigades. If there was to be an envelopment of the Union left, Law's and Benning's Brigades were the only ones potentially in position to do so. However, the combined Law-Benning decisions negated even that possibility as the combat power that was initially in the right of Hood's attack was shifted toward his division's center. There they struck head-on Union forces in a defensive position, rather than striking an overwhelming blow on the flank of the defenses.

Greene Remains on Culp's Hill

When the Army of the Potomac's final position was established in the evening hours of July 1 and morning of July 2, the right (north) flank was on Culp's Hill. This hill was a natural position for the right flank as it protected and supported that part of the defensive position on Cemetery Hill, prevented entry into the army's rear area behind Cemetery Ridge, and protected the Baltimore Pike, which was one of Meade's major supply routes. The capture of Culp's Hill by a large Confederate force would give Lee a tactical advantage that could cause the disruption of Meade's position and perhaps a Confederate victory.

The first defenders on Culp's Hill were the remainder of Brigadier General James S. Wadsworth's First Division, First Corps. On the first day Wadsworth's division had been involved in the heavy fighting along McPherson's and Seminary Ridges. After retreating from its earlier positions, the division, what was left of it, went into position on the northern side of Culp's Hill. There they established a defensive position that went from west to east and faced north. They provided mutual support to and in turn were supported by the infantry and artillery on East Cemetery Hill.[34]

The Twelfth Corps arrived on the battlefield late on July 1. One division, Brigadier General Alpheus S. Williams's First Division, was positioned east of Rock Creek and north of the Baltimore Pike. The other division, Brigadier General John W. Geary's Second Division, was positioned to the right (north) of Little Round Top. Both divisions spent the night in these locations and early the next morning were ordered to Culp's Hill.[35]

Geary's division went into position to the right of Wadsworth's and was oriented to the northeast and east. The left brigade of the division was Brigadier General George S. Greene's Third Brigade. Brigadier General Thomas L. Kane's Second Brigade was to Greene's right. Colonel Charles Candy's First Brigade occupied a supporting position behind Greene. Geary's position went from the top of the Culp's Hill south for 1,100 yards.

Williams's division (later commanded by Brigadier General Thomas Ruger while Williams was temporarily in command of the corps), on Geary's right, extended the position another 500 yards south; then the line bent back so as to face south and went west for 500 yards to the Baltimore Pike. With Wadsworth's division and Geary's and Williams's divisions of the Twelfth Corps, Meade's right flank on Culp's Hill was a tight and compact defensive position which was strengthened by the troops constructing breastworks.[36]

At sixty-two years of age, George S. Greene was the oldest general officer at Gettys-

Brigadier General George S. Greene. U.S. Army Military History Institute.

burg. Graduating from West Point in 1823, he served in the army until 1836, when he resigned and became a civil engineer. He rejoined the army in January 1862 as a colonel and was promoted to brigadier general in April. Prior to Gettysburg he had fought at Cedar Mountain, Antietam, and Chancellorsville.[37]

Greene's five-regiment brigade was the left flank brigade of the Twelfth Corps. Greene's initial position was 550 yards long. His left regiment was on the apex of Culp's Hill. Three more regiments occupied positions to the right (south) of that regiment. A fifth regiment was deployed as a skirmish line in front of the brigade. Little did Greene or his men realize the critical role they would perform later in the day.[38]

At dawn on July 2, two divisions of Ewell's Corps faced Culp's Hill. Major General Jubal A. Early's division was on the southeastern edge of Gettysburg, approximately 650 yards north of the hill. To Early's left rear (northeast), Major General Edward Johnson's division was 1,500 yards north of Culp's Hill.[39]

Lee's plan of attack for July 2 was for Longstreet, with two of his divisions, to envelop Meade's south flank. Anderson's Division of Hill's Corps would support Longstreet and attack on his left. At the same time, Ewell was ordered to conduct a demonstration and, if an opportunity presented itself, to turn this into an attack on Meade's right flank on East Cemetery Hill and Culp's Hill. Lee's intention was for Ewell to hold the Union troops on Culp's Hill in position so that Meade would not be able to redeploy them to reinforce his left or left center.[40]

When Longstreet made contact with Sickles's Third Corps at the Peach Orchard, his artillery deployed and opened fire. This was the signal for Ewell to begin his demonstration. Major Joseph Latimer's artillery battalion was deployed to Benner's Hill and opened fire on the Union positions on East Cemetery Hill. Union artillery on Cemetery Hill and Culp's Hill placed such accurate fire on Latimer's position that most of his guns were withdrawn and Latimer was mortally wounded. Ewell followed up the artillery demonstration with an attack by two of Early's brigades against East Cemetery Hill while Johnson's Division attacked Culp's Hill.[41]

However, Johnson's attack was too late, and Meade had done exactly what Lee wanted to prevent. During the attack by Longstreet's Corps and Anderson's Division, a serious situation began developing in the left center of Meade's position on Cemetery Ridge. To reinforce the defenders in this area, Meade ordered the Twelfth Corps to depart Culp's Hill and reinforce the left center of his position.[42]

Williams's division, under Ruger's command and the right flank of the Twelfth Corps, departed Culp's Hill some time after 6:00 p.m. This left

Geary's division as the only Twelfth Corps unit defending the east side of the hill. Approximately thirty minutes later, Geary received orders to follow Ruger and reinforce the army's left flank. There are several versions as to what happened next. In one version Slocum sent his adjutant general, Colonel Hiram C. Rodgers, to Meade's headquarters, seeking permission to keep Geary's division in its defensive position. Meade believed the most dangerous threat was on his left and left center; however, he gave permission for Slocum to leave one brigade on Culp's Hill. Slocum then sent Rodgers to Geary with instruction to leave Greene's brigade on the hill while the remainder of the division moved to reinforce the left. In another version Geary received the order to march his entire division to reinforce the left and left center. When all three brigades were in the process of forming up to move, the advance units of Johnson's attack made contact with Greene's skirmish line, and he was warned of the approaching attack. Greene then halted his brigade's preparations to move, redeployed into a defensive posture, and extended his line to the right to cover as much terrain as possible. About the same time, Rodgers arrived with Slocum's instruction. In all probability both versions entwine with each other, and the discrepancy is caused by the participants's different perspectives. The important point is, whether by Greene's or Slocum's decision, a brigade remained in defensive positions on Culp's Hill.[43]

On Culp's Hill the responsibility to defend what only an hour before had been covered by two divisions presented Greene with an almost impossible situation: he had insufficient troops to defend the entire vacated position. However, he could defend the left part and the hill's apex. Greene accomplished this by thinning out his line and extending his defenses to the right.[44]

Johnson's Division was composed of four brigades. Johnson deployed three of his brigades east of Culp's Hill and at 7:00 P.M. sent them forward against Greene's defenses. In the gathering darkness, Johnson's right and center brigades (Jones's and Nicholls's) struck Greene's defenses, while the left brigade (Steuart's) began to envelop Greene's right flank. This potentially deadly threat to the defenders was stopped when Greene's right flank was refused and reinforcements arrived. By 10:00 P.M. the Confederate attack had come to a halt.[45]

Had not Greene's brigade remained on Culp's Hill, in all probability Johnson's Division would have captured the position. Even though Wadsworth's division was there, it was oriented to the north and would have had extreme difficulty in reorienting against an attack from the east in time to be effective.

Greene's successful defense kept Johnson's attack from capturing the key terrain on Meade's extreme right. Had this position been lost, it would

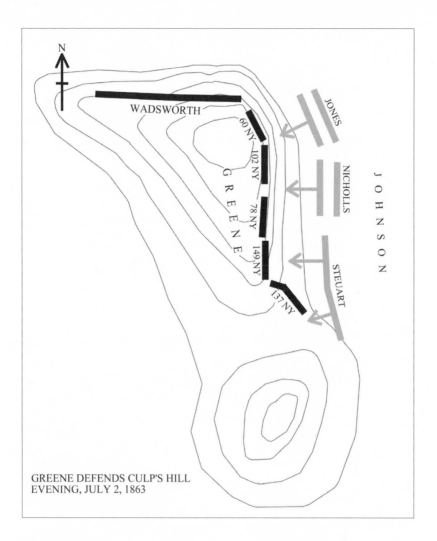

GREENE DEFENDS CULP'S HILL
EVENING, JULY 2, 1863

have opened the way for the capture of the Baltimore Pike and placed a large Confederate force in the Army of the Potomac's rear area.

The battle in the area of Culp's Hill proceeded as it did because of the decision to keep Greene's brigade there. The impact of this decision carried into the next day and shaped Lee's decisions for July 3. After the fighting died out on the night of July 2, the position provided an anchor for a continuation of the battle the next day.

Seven Confederate brigades, Johnson's four and three reinforcing (two from Rodes and one from Early), were committed to the fight for Culp's Hill in the morning hours of July 3. This sizable force was not available to reinforce or support Lee's attack on Meade's center later in the day.[46]

CHAPTER 4

FRIDAY, JULY 3, 1863, AND AFTERWARD

One of Lee's objectives in moving his army out of Virginia was to fight and defeat the Army of the Potomac on Northern territory. In the last days of June, he began concentrating his army for the decisive battle he sought. However, with Stuart out of contact and unable to communicate with him, this concentration was being done with minimal information on where Meade's army was located.

During the process of concentrating, Lee's army made contact with the lead elements of Meade's army on July 1. The failure of subordinates to follow their commander's intent, concentrate, and then fight, along with poor decision-making, brought four divisions into a battle that Lee was not prepared to fight until at least the following day.

Unwillingly committed to battle on July 1, Lee decided he must make the best of the situation. Unable to remain east of South Mountain and the Cumberland Valley for an extended period of time and unwilling to withdraw and surrender the initiative, he found that his only option was to attack. This he proceeded to do on Thursday.

Lee's July 2 plan was for a main attack against the Union left with a supporting attack against Meade's right. This plan was based on poor reconnaissance by his staff and subordinates and no reconnaissance from his absent cavalry.

Even though the supporting attack provided no timely assistance to the main attack, it was partially successful on its own. The partial successes of the main and supporting attacks caused Lee to think that a coordinate action by his army could still produce the victory he sought and so desperately needed.

Slocum and Williams Steal the Initiative

On July 2 Longstreet, using two of his divisions, was to conduct an envelopment and attack Meade's left (south) flank. This was the main attack. Simultaneously Ewell was to conduct a demonstration, with the option of turning it into an attack, on Meade's right (north) flank. This was the supporting attack. Ewell's supporting attack was to hold the Union troops in positions on Cemetery Hill and Culp's Hill to prevent Meade from moving them south to reinforce his position there. Because of a lack of coordination, poor staff work, and difficulties in communication between the two flanks, Ewell's attack did not begin as soon as it should have and did not keep all of the defenders in place.[1]

Ewell began his demonstration with Major Joseph W. Latimer's reinforced artillery battalion. Latimer deployed twenty guns on to Benner's Hill, twelve hundred yards north-northeast of Culp's Hill and seventeen hundred yards northeast of East Cemetery Hill, and engaged in an artillery duel with the Union batteries on East Cemetery Hill. Latimer opened fire shortly after Longstreet's artillery began firing on the south flank. Latimer's gunners held their position for two hours but were eventually forced off Benner's Hill by the artillery on East Cemetery Hill.[2]

Ewell followed up his artillery demonstration with two infantry attacks: one against East Cemetery Hill and one against Culp's Hill. Two brigades from Early's Division made the attack against East Cemetery Hill. After heavy fighting, this attack was repulsed by the Eleventh Corps with reinforcements from the Second Corps. Major General Edward Johnson's division conducted the attack against Culp's Hill. Earlier in the day Culp's Hill was defended by the first day's survivors of Brigadier General James Wadsworth's division of the First Corps and the two divisions of the Twelfth Corps.[3]

Prior to Ewell's ordering his infantry attacks, Meade did exactly what Lee was trying to prevent and redeployed most of the Twelfth Corps off of Culp's Hill to provide reinforcements to the left and left center part of his defenses, then under heavy attack. When Johnson commenced his attack, only Wadsworth's troops and Brigadier General George S. Greene's brigade were on Culp's Hill.[4]

Extending his brigade to occupy as much of the unmanned Twelfth Corps position as possible, Greene, eventually reinforced with other regiments, fought a masterful defensive action and was able to hold the higher part of the hill while having to give up the lower southeastern part. Although denied the top of the hill, Johnson controlled the lower southern section. With darkness and the end of fighting, Johnson had units within six hundred yards of the Baltimore Pike and in an excellent position to renew his attack and capture this critical Union supply and communications route.[5]

On the third day Lee initially planned to conduct a double envelopment against both flanks of Meade's position. This was to be a coordinated continuation of the attacks that Longstreet and Ewell had begun the day before. To strengthen both attacks, two brigades from Rodes's Division and one brigade from Early's Division reinforced Johnson while Longstreet would have Pickett's Division available.[6]

The Twelfth Corps was temporarily commanded by Brigadier General Alpheus S. Williams while Major General Henry W. Slocum acted as the right-wing commander and coordinated the movement of forces on the right of the army. A graduate of Yale University in 1831, Williams spent the next thirty years as a lawyer, probate judge, newspaper owner, and the postmaster of Detroit. During the Mexican War he served as the lieutenant colonel of a Michigan regiment. President of the state military board in 1861,

he went on active duty in August as a brigadier general. Prior to Gettysburg he had been in combat in the Shenandoah Valley, Cedar Mountain, Antietam, and Chancellorsville. Williams's immediate superior and normally the corps commander was Henry W. Slocum.[7]

An 1852 West Point graduate, Slocum resigned his commission four years later to practice law. Returning to military service in 1861 as colonel of the Twenty-seventh New York, he rapidly rose through brigade and division command to become commander of the Twelfth Corps in late 1862. A veteran of First Bull Run, the Peninsula Campaign, Second Bull Run,

Brigadier General Alpheus S. Williams. U.S. Army Military History Institute

the 1862 Maryland Campaign, and Chancellorsville, he brought considerable combat experience to Gettysburg.[8]

During the night, when the first elements of the Twelfth Corps tried to return to Culp's Hill, they discovered their positions were controlled by Johnson's troops. That night, as the acting corps commander, Williams attended Meade's commanders meeting. On returning to his corps, he was informed that Confederates occupied part of their previous defensive position. Reporting this information to Slocum at about midnight, Williams was ordered to drive the enemy from the entrenchments

Major General Henry W. Slocum. National Archives.

at daylight. What happened next severely limited Lee's options for July 3, had a decisive impact on the final day of battle, and shaped the final day of combat.[9]

Returning to his corps, Williams immediately began to position artillery and infantry for an attack. Five batteries of artillery were placed in firing positions south and west of Culp's Hill. From their positions on Powers Hill and along the Baltimore Pike, the artillery was able to provide fire support for the infantry attack. As the artillery was moved into position, the infantry deployed into attack formation south and west of the hill. When the sky began to lighten with the approaching day, the Union force went into action with a pre-assault artillery bombardment followed by an infantry attack. This artillery fire caught Johnson completely by surprise. Preparing to initiate his own attack and not expecting the aggressive Union action, Johnson immediately ordered his division to commence its attack. The Twelfth Corps units quickly went over to the defense. For the next six hours, soldiers on both sides were locked in a desperate struggle for control of Culp's Hill, which was the key to the right of Meade's position. By 10:30 A.M., even though Johnson's brigades had fought themselves to exhaustion, Culp's Hill remained in the hands of the almost equally exhausted defenders. As Johnson withdrew his brigades, the Twelfth Corps reoccupied their original positions on lower Culp's Hill.[10]

Slocum's order to "drive them out at first light" and Williams's immediate preparations to position his artillery and infantry for an attack at first light took the initiative away from Ewell and Johnson. Although Johnson was also prepared to attack at first light, Williams's artillery preparation before the attack forced him into ordering his brigades forward. When Ewell received word that Lee had postponed the early morning attack, it was too late to stop Johnson's attack. More important, once Johnson's units became decisively engaged, Williams's aggressiveness precluded the possibility of Johnson's breaking contact and withdrawing in order to be available to support the afternoon Confederate attack against Meade's center. By the time Lee began to formulate his final plan for July 3, the left of his line had been decisively engaged and repulsed with such losses as to render the force unusable for the rest of the day. This severely limited the resources Lee had available for any offensive action he might choose.

Lee Attacks the Union Center

As darkness fell on the night of July 2, Lee must have felt that victory was almost within his grasp. He could look back on the events of the day and attribute the failure of his army to have won the battle to a lack of coordinated action by all of his corps.

Following this line of thought, his initial plan for the third day was a continuation of the previous day's plan. Now that Major General George Pickett's division had rejoined the army, he would reinforce Longstreet's other two divisions, and all three would continue the attack on Meade's south flank. Part of Hill's Corps would conduct a supporting attack on Longstreet's left. On the north flank, Ewell would renew his attacks against the right of Meade's position. Major General J. E. B. Stuart, who had finally rejoined the army, was ordered to position his cavalry on the army's left. From there it could attack the Union rear or exploit any collapse of Meade's defensive line. No sooner had the orders for this plan been delivered than it began to fall apart.[11]

There was no meeting between Lee and his corps commanders on the night of July 2—but there should have been. Lee did not call his corps commanders to his headquarters, and none of them took it upon themselves to go there. Longstreet should have gone to Lee's headquarters to discuss his reservations about Lee's initial July 3 plan. Such a meeting could have accomplished the coordination necessary to carry out Lee's plan. More important, an accurate assessment as to the strength and disposition of Longstreet's divisions could have been presented. This would have allowed time for modifications to Lee's plan or for a new plan to have been developed and coordinated. Barring any communications from his corps commanders, Lee had every expectation that preparations were being made to continue the attack early the next morning.

Early on the morning of July 3, Lee rode to the southern part of his position, probably near the Peach Orchard, to confer with Longstreet. During this meeting Longstreet informed Lee that he could not carry out his portion of the plan. Not only had McLaws's and Hood's Divisions taken so many casualties on the previous day that they did not have the strength to attack, but to their front the Union troops had been reinforced and had strengthened their positions. Not only could they not attack, but also he was not sure of being able to hold the ground that they had gained if they were counterattacked. Longstreet also pointed out that, if he continued his attack toward the northeast, he would leave a large enemy force behind him that might come down off the Round Tops and attack him in the rear. Lee conceded to Longstreet's points and canceled his initial plan. As this was happening on the south flank, Johnson's reinforced division was decisively committed to a battle for Culp's Hill. By the time Lee had formulated his second plan for July 3, Johnson's force was fought out and could not be included in any offensive operation Lee might decide on.[12]

With his initial third-day plan falling apart, Lee was again faced with the three tactical options available to any commander. He could attack, defend, or move away from the enemy. Lee did not believe that he could afford to maintain a defensive position east of South Mountain. He was concerned about supplying his army over a limited road system while east of the mountain. There was also the possibility that Meade might maneuver a force between him and the mountain passes or even across his routes of communication and supply in the Cumberland Valley. Lee also believed that Meade could probably outwait him if he went on the defense. Lee had brought the Army of Northern Virginia north in order to defeat the Army of the Potomac on Northern soil, hoping thereby to gain a political advantage. To move away from Meade—in other words, retreat—would be to give up this one particular objective of the campaign.[13]

When Lee moved north into Maryland and Pennsylvania, he had disrupted, for that summer, any major operational plans the Union had in mind in Virginia. He subsisted his army by foraging on Northern territory and gathering additional supplies, food, and forage to help supply his army after it returned to Virginia. If he retreated now, only two of the campaign objectives would have been attained.[14]

While accomplishing these two campaign objectives was noteworthy, it was not decisive in the overall strategic situation. For his campaign to be decisive, it must advance the Confederacy's political objective. Anything less would maintain the strategic situation in the East as it had been after the Battle of Chancellorsville. Therefore, Lee concluded, he had only one option: he must attack. The only question that remained was where.

Lee's options as to the location of the attack were limited. The day before, Lee had planned an envelopment of Meade's south flank. Longstreet with two of his divisions, supported by Anderson's Division from Hill's Corps, had conducted the main attack. Ewell was simultaneously to conduct a supporting attack with elements of Early's and Johnston's Divisions. Lee's plan had been flawed, the coordination of the attacks had failed, and the result had been less than intended. His initial plan for the next day was to be a double envelopment of Meade's defenses. Longstreet with all three of his divisions was to attack Meade's south flank while simultaneously Johnson's Division, reinforced with three additional brigades, was to attack the north flank. This plan collapsed after Lee's early morning meeting with Longstreet. He canceled the attack on the left part of the Union position because of the condition of his force there. By then Johnson's forces had attacked Meade's right flank and become decisively engaged. This attack continued until midmorning without any positive results. Had Lee been able to stop this attack, it might have been an option for the main attack if it were properly reinforced. Or the troops could have been used to support or reinforce his main attack once Lee decided where it would be. However, none of these options were open to him.[15]

Major General George Pickett's division was the only division that had not fought on the previous two days. Longstreet's other two divisions, Hood's and McLaws's, had taken significant casualties the day before. In Ewell's Corps, Rodes's Division had seen heavy fighting on July 1, and two of his brigades had been used to reinforce Johnson for his first light attack on July 3. In the attack on East Cemetery Hill, two of Early's brigades were involved in significant fighting, and a third brigade had been sent to reinforce Johnson. This left only Hill's Corps from which to draw forces to attack with Pickett. Anderson's Division had participated in the attack the day before, with several brigades taking casualties. Heth's and Pender's Divisions had both done heavy fighting on July 1 but had not significantly participated during the attack on July 2.[16]

Taken all together, these parameters limited Lee's options to one choice: an attack in the center. For this he used Pickett's previously uncommitted division with three brigades, four brigades of Heth's Division, two brigades of Pender's Division, and two brigades of Anderson's Division, with the last eight brigades all from Hill's Corps. Preceding the attack would be an artillery preparation using most of the guns of Longstreet's and Hill's Corps and as many guns from Ewell's as could range on Meade's defenses. Lee's tactical objective was to break the Union defenses along Cemetery Ridge, as represented by the "Copse of Trees." If successful this would split Meade's army and control one of the supply routes, the Taneytown Road. Such a situation would leave Meade with one of two options—a counterattack to restore the position or a retreat to reunite his army.[17]

Lee's decision may have also been influenced by the accomplishments of Brigadier General Ambrose R. Wright's brigade. Late in the afternoon of the second day, Wright's Brigade, of Anderson's Division, was supporting Longstreet's attack. Wright attacked from his location in the center of the Confederate position on Seminary Ridge. His brigade moved over open ground, crossed the Emmitsburg Road, and attacked the Union position just south of the clump of trees made famous by the next day's attack. Wright's Brigade was able to penetrate the defensive position at this point, but being unsupported on his flanks and needing reinforcement, he was unable to hold what he had gained. Part of Wright's success can be attributed to the lateral movement of Union forces from the center of the line to positions farther south. Even though other units were being moved to cover the center part of the line, they had not arrived prior to Wright's attack. Wright's temporary success must have helped Lee arrive at the decision to attack what he thought was the weakly held center of Meade's line. For a time Lee's assumption was correct: the center was vulnerable. But by midmorning on July 3 it was not.[18]

The previous night Meade was informed by Colonel George H. Sharpe, the head of his intelligence service, the Bureau of Military Information, that Lee's only uncommitted unit was Pickett's Division. Sharpe's order of battle for Lee's army had several mistakes. It showed Pickett with four brigades rather than the three that were at Gettysburg; one brigade had remained in Virginia. Rodes's Division was shown with four brigades rather than five, as Daniel's Brigade had not been identified. However, it was a remarkable analysis that provided Meade with important intelligence at the right time.[19]

Later on that night Meade told Brigadier General John Gibbon, "If Lee attacks tomorrow, it will be on your front. Because he had made attacks on both our flanks and failed and if he concludes to try it again, it will be in our center." The Copse of Trees was in the center of Gibbon's division's position. Early on the morning of July 3, Meade had his chief of staff send a message to Major General John Sedgwick, commander of the Sixth Corps, directing that two brigades be moved into a reserve position behind the center of the Union line, which Sedgwick did. Additionally Meade had his chief of artillery, Brigadier General Henry Hunt, inspect the artillery positions from Cemetery Hill to Little Round Top, with instructions to make any changes he saw fit. During this inspection Hunt saw the Confederate artillery moving into position and correctly assumed that the Union center was about to be attacked. At the same time that Lee was changing his plan from a double envelopment to a frontal attack against Meade's center, Meade had already completed his analysis and was making preparation to defeat just such an attack.[20]

The results of Lee's decision are well known. The final attempt to break Meade's position began with the largest artillery bombardment and counter-bombardment ever conducted on the North American continent. After two hours it was followed by the infantry attack. The Pickett-Pettigrew-Trimble attack was made and repulsed with heavy loss. Many of the regiments in Pettigrew's and Trimble's commands had taken casualties on the first day of fighting. After the third day's attack, they were severely depleted in combat power. Pickett's division was wrecked in the attack. Thus, as a result of this decision, every one of Lee's divisions had seen heavy fighting and taken severe casualties. With his combat power greatly reduced, Lee would be forced into one more major decision.

Lee Retreats from Gettysburg

The repulse of the Confederate attack on the afternoon of July 3 brought the majority of the fighting to a close. It also placed Lee and Meade in the position of making major decisions that shaped the remainder of the campaign.

During the night Ewell's Corps moved from its locations in and east of Gettysburg to a position on Seminary Ridge that was north of Hill's Corps. On the south flank Longstreet's divisions were withdrawn to positions along Seminary Ridge. These moves brought Lee's army into a compact and continuous defensive position on Seminary Ridge.[21]

Various sources calculate Lee's casualties at Gettysburg from 20,451 to 28,000 men in killed, wounded, and captured, or approximately 27 percent to 37 percent of his army's strength. That said, 25,747 seems to be the best figure for the three days of battle. Among these were 4 division commanders, 16 brigade commanders, and 91 regimental commanders or their replacements—the equivalent of a corps command structure. The losses in commanders and soldiers during the three days of fighting had considerably reduced the strength and combat power of his army. Ammunition expenditure had been high. The firing of almost twenty-two thousand rounds of artillery and millions of rounds of small arms ammunition had cut deep into the army's ordnance supplies. Estimates were that there was sufficient ammunition left for one more day of battle. The reduced strength of his army and the ammunition expenditure precluded Lee from considering another attack. His options now were defense or retreat.[22]

Most of the rations carried by his soldiers through South Mountain from the Cumberland Valley had been consumed, and with all divisions now deployed there was no opportunity to resupply or gather additional supplies. Even if they could forage, the area east of the mountain that was controlled by Lee's army was foraged out. In addition, sources of water were drying up. There were no major rivers in the area, and wells had been drawn from until they were dry; the streams in the area could not make up the difference.

In addition, Lee was concerned that Meade might attempt to maneuver a force to block the mountain passes in his rear. He might also steal a march on Lee and move significant forces south and then west into the Cumberland Valley and block the return route to Virginia. The analysis of all these factors could only bring Lee to the conclusion that he must retreat or run the unacceptable risk of having his army rendered combat ineffective.[23]

Throughout Saturday, July 4, Lee continued to occupy his defensive position on Seminary Ridge while preparing to retreat. Remaining in position for one more day provided Lee the opportunity to collect many of his wounded, place them in wagons, and start them on the journey back to Virginia. The recovery of his wounded, in time, provided a pool of veteran replacements as their wounds healed and they rejoined the army.[24]

Lee may have hoped that Meade would order his army to attack the Army of Northern Virginia. Situated in well-established defensive positions, all the advantages of a defender's firepower against a foe advancing over open ground would be Lee's. He may have thought that if Meade were to do this, his army would inflict heavy casualties on the attackers and gain some semblance of victory. However, this was not to be, and on Saturday night the Army of Northern Virginia began the retreat from Gettysburg.[25]

Meade also faced a serious decision on the afternoon of July 3. With the repulse of the Confederate attack, should he counterattack? Meade's decision was not to follow up with an immediate counterattack. Lee at the same time was rallying his troops into defensive positions in expectation of such an attack.[26]

Meade's army was fought out after three days of heavy fighting, which was preceded by many days of hard forced-marching. Throughout July 4 he continued to maintain a defensive posture and conduct limited resupply. Meade's losses had also been severe. Twenty-four percent, 23,049 solders, of the Army of the Potomac, had been killed, wounded, or captured. Among them were 3 corps commanders, 3 division commanders, 17 brigade commanders, and 100 regimental commander or their replacements. Sixty-one percent of the casualties were from the First, Third, and Eleventh Corps, rendering them temporarily ineffective for sustained offensive operations. As with the Confederates, the Army of the Potomac had expended vast amounts of small arms and artillery ammunition, 32,781 rounds for the artillery. In addition, this was the first major victory the Army of the Potomac had enjoyed in almost a year. Meade also realized the advantages of the defense and saw no reason to give Lee a chance to recover victory from defeat.[27]

Taken together, the decisions of both commanders would bring an end to the fighting around Gettysburg. Had Lee attempted to continue the offense or had Meade switched from the defense to the offense, then the bloody contest would have gone on for another day. The results of another day of fighting and what would have happened on the days after can only be surmised. Would we be reading that Lee's army was broken by Union attacks; that Meade, having won a masterful victory, threw it away with fruitless attacks on Lee's position; or that the Army of the Potomac was again in retreat away from the enemy after having suffered unacceptable losses? The decisions made by Lee and Meade removed these scenarios from history and shaped the last part of the campaign—the return to Virginia.

CONCLUSION

Lee issued orders to his army on the afternoon of July 4, Saturday, for the retreat from Gettysburg. Hill's Corps moved first, followed by Longstreet's and then Ewell's, which was the rear guard. The corps were to march on the Fairfield-Hagerstown Road through Monterey Pass in South Mountain, on to Hagerstown, and then Williamsport, where they would cross the Potomac River into Virginia. When Hill's Corps reached the approach to the gap in the mountain, it was to take up a defensive position facing east while the rest of the army continued on into the Cumberland Valley. Hill would then follow as the rear guard. The divisional trains of Longstreet's and Hill's Corps were to march in the middle of the infantry column.[1]

Prior to the movement of the infantry corps, there were two large trains that departed the Gettysburg area. The first train to depart was the reserve train, sometimes referred to as Ewell's Corps train. This train, under the command of Major John H. Harmon, contained much of the supplies, forage, and subsistence, including beef animals on the hoof that had been taken by Ewell's foragers since they had been in Pennsylvania. Located in the vicinity of Fairfield, it departed at 3:00 A.M. on July 4, with the last wagons on the road by 1:00 P.M. The divisional trains of Ewell's Corps immediately followed it. The divisional trains carried supplies, ammunition, and wounded. These two combined trains occupied a road space of approximately forty miles. After passing through South Mountain at Monterey Pass, they continued on to Williamsport, where they planned to cross the Potomac River into Virginia.[2]

The second large train, occupying a road space of seventeen miles, was composed primarily of wounded. Escorted by Brigadier General John D. Imboden's cavalry brigade, it departed from the vicinity of Cashtown on Saturday at 4:00 P.M., using the Chambersburg Pike. Its planned route was west through South Mountain, then south down the Cumberland Valley, across the Potomac River at Williamsport, and on to Winchester, Virginia, where the army was to join them. Approximately 8,500 wounded were carried in these two trains while 6,802 wounded who could not travel were left behind and captured by Meade's soldiers.[3]

The infantry began their retreat at dark with Hill's Corps departing Seminary Ridge, later followed by Longstreet's Corps. Because of heavy rains and a deteriorating road, progress was not as fast as planned for, and Ewell's Corps did not begin to march until almost noon on July 5. However, the army did successfully cross South Mountain and was in the vicinity of Hagerstown on July 7. From Hagerstown, Lee planned to continue on to Williamsport and cross the Potomac River. However, the bridge at Williamsport had been destroyed, and the heavy rains that hampered the retreat had also raised the water level of the Potomac River. Lee had no choice but to order his army and the trains into a defensive position on the north side of the Potomac and wait for the water level to recede.[4]

Meade sent his cavalry against the Confederate trains as Lee began his retreat. The off and on clashes between Union cavalry and Confederate forces characterized the retreat. Meade held his infantry in position at Gettysburg until a reconnaissance in force by part of the Sixth Corps on Sunday, July 5, confirmed that Lee had departed Seminary Ridge and was retreating along the road to Hagerstown. Meade responded by moving his army south on routes east of South Mountain and by Tuesday was concentrated in the vicinity of Middletown, Maryland—eight miles west of Frederick. The next day his forces crossed South Mountain on roads and through gaps used the previous year en route to Antietam. July 9 found the Union army in the Cumberland Valley just east of Hagerstown. The next two days were spent in a cautious approach toward Lee's defenses. On Sunday, July 12, Meade began preparation for an attack on Lee's position. The next day he conducted a personal reconnaissance and ordered an attack for the following day. When Union troops moved forward, they found the position abandoned. The majority of Lee's army had crossed over the river the previous night. Only a rear guard remained north of the Potomac. Its clash with part of Meade's cavalry prior to crossing was the final fight of the campaign.[5]

On July 24 the Army of Northern Virginia began arriving at Culpeper Court House just twenty-three miles west of Chancellorsville. Lee's army was where it had begun the campaign, forty-five days before. Meade's Army of the Potomac followed Lee's across the Potomac River, returned to Virginia, and occupied positions along the line of the Rappahannock River. The Gettysburg Campaign was over.[6]

Lee had gone north in the summer of 1863 to accomplish three objectives. He wanted to influence the political situation, subsist his army on Northern territory, and disrupt any major Union campaign plans in Virginia. Lee failed to accomplish his political objective. It would have required a clear-cut victory over the Army of the Potomac somewhere in Maryland or Pennsylvania for his campaign to have an adverse political effect in the North. The Confederate victory never came about.

Lee successfully accomplished his other two objectives. Although the Battles of Fredericksburg and Chancellorsville had been Confederate victories, Lee saw them as only preserving the status quo. At Fredericksburg, Lee had inflicted 12,653 casualties on the Army of the Potomac for a cost to his army of 4,201. At Chancellorsville, Lee had caused 17,287 Union casualties for 10,281 in his army. However, each time his opponent had been able to secure relative safety by retreating back across the Rappahannock River, leaving the tactical situation as it had been before the battles. Lee saw that this continual response to his opponent's initiative, even if he was tactically successful, would result only in the weakening of his army to the point that failure on the battlefield was a real future possibility. To break the cycle of responding to Union initiatives, Lee decided to take the initiative and move first. In this he was successful, and the commanders of the Army of the Potomac were prevented from developing or initiating a campaign plan that summer and were forced to conform to Lee's maneuvering.[7]

Lee met total success in the accomplishment of his objective to feed his army off the farms in Maryland and Pennsylvania. The feeding of Lee's soldiers and horses had been particularly hard during the winter of 1862–63. Meat and other foodstuffs were less and less available to the soldiers. As a result Lee had sent Longstreet with two divisions to southeastern Virginia and had moved many of the army's horses away from the army to where forage might be found. By the spring of 1863 there appeared to be no improvement in the situation. Lee's invasion into the North moved his army into an area rich in food and forage that subsisted his army. In addition, he was able to bring back to Virginia not only food, including large herds of cows and sheep, but all manner of material and supplies that would help keep his army in the field.[8]

However, Lee paid a high cost to accomplish these two objectives. He began the campaign (depending on the source) with between 75,000 and

80,000 infantrymen, artillerymen, and cavalrymen. Casualties were 25,747. Among these were 5,000 dead, 5,445 missing, and 6,802 captured. These figures represent a permanent loss to Lee's army of 17,247 soldiers. Of the 8,500 wounded brought back to Virginia, some later died (adding to the death rates), others were invalid and discharged, and some returned to the army to fight again. By the spring of 1864 Lee's army had recovered some of its strength and numbered 61,953. Even more troublesome for Lee was the loss in leadership among his combat units, including 4 division commanders, 16 brigade commanders, and 91 regimental commanders or their replacements—the equivalent of a corps command structure. In addition, desertions became such a problem that Lee issued a general amnesty to entice solders to return to the army.[9]

In the spring of 1864 Meade's army, under the close supervision of Lieutenant General Ulysses S. Grant, commenced a series of tactical maneuvers and battles that moved both armies toward and then south of Richmond. Grant was doing what Lee had done before. He grasped the initiative and started the campaign in Virginia before Lee could begin operations. Once he had the initiative, Grant never let it go as he kept the Union forces in Virginia in close contact with Lee's army and other Confederate forces. This continual tempo of offensive operations never gave Lee the opportunity to go over to the offense as he had the previous two years. Without offensive opportunities Lee had no chance to move the fighting into northern Virginia or farther north. The repeated cycles of combat and then maneuver by both armies ended when the Army of Northern Virginia entered the defensive lines at Petersburg. From that point on, the end was just a matter of time. It came in April 1865.

The Gettysburg campaign and battle went into the history books. But it has not been forgotten, far from it. Probably more has been written about Gettysburg than any other battle in U.S. history. The writings, discussions, and arguments began almost immediately after the war, have carried on until today, and will go into the future. Some believe it was the "high water mark" of the Confederacy, while at the other end of the spectrum there are those who believe it did not matter at all. In between these two positions there is a multitude of beliefs. Some believe that it ended the last chance the Confederacy had to obtain a negotiated peace. Others view it as the event that decided the Confederacy could not win the war in the East, but could lose it there. Some see it in the context of Grant's victory at Vicksburg and the fighting in central Tennessee and northern Georgia that followed later in the summer. Whatever one's position on Gettysburg is, it was the nineteen decisions presented here that shaped the campaign and the battle.

Lee's decision to retreat from Gettysburg brought the cycle of decisions full circle. The first decision was to march north into Pennsylvania; the last was to march south back to Virginia. The first and the last decisions were strategic decisions. There were two organizational decisions—reorganization of the Army of Northern Virginia and reorganization of the artillery of the Army of the Potomac. The other fifteen decisions were all tactical. Of the tactical decisions, three were army level, six were corps level, three were divisional level, and three were made at brigade level of command.

The three army-level decisions were Meade's to move his army to Gettysburg and Lee's to continue offensive operations on July 2 and to attack in the center on July 3. Reynolds's decision to reinforce Buford, Ewell's decision not to attack Cemetery Hill on the first day, Sickles's to move forward to the Peach Orchard, Longstreet's to countermarch and attack on the Union left, and Slocum's to attack on Culp's Hill were the corps level decisions. The divisional-level decisions were Stuart's, Rodes's, and Buford's. Law, Benning, and Greene made the three critical decisions at brigade level.

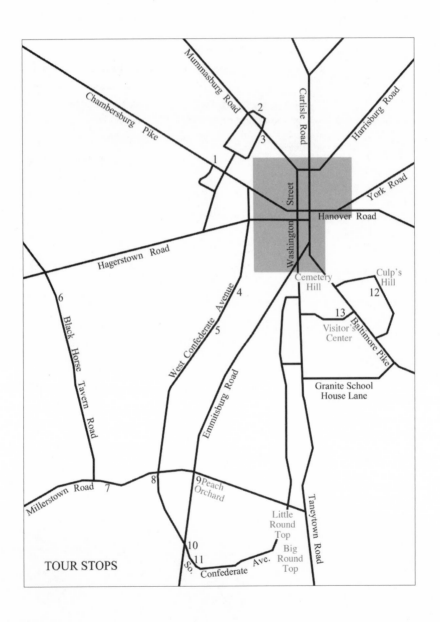

APPENDIX I

A BATTLEFIELD GUIDE TO THE CRITICAL DECISIONS AT GETTYSBURG

There is value in being in close proximity to where a decision was made or carried out. Being on the ground provides a perspective that can't be gained through reading or map study. In some cases this is not feasible—if you are at Gettysburg, for example, and the decision was made in Richmond or somewhere else in Virginia. Most of the critical decisions presented in this book were made and carried out at Gettysburg. Starting with the events of July 1, this appendix provides a battlefield tour that will place you on the ground exactly or in close proximity to where critical decisions were made and/or carried out.

The tour is designed on a geographical basis, rather than in strict chronological order. This prevents you from having to circle back around on different days to locations that are in proximity to each other. Nevertheless, for the most part it is in chronological order.

If you wish for more detail about the decisions than is provided in the guide, read the decisions discussions in the appropriate chapters.

There are parking areas at most of the stops. Where there is not, park on the right half of the road. As most roads are one-way, cars will be able to pass by. Do not pull off the roads and park on the shoulders.

Grammatical use and spelling were often different in the 1860s from today. However, I have left quoted material from the participants as they wrote it—for example: Emmitsburg *road* in the 1860s, Emmitsburg *Road* today; *reenforce* or *re-enforce* in the 1860s, *reinforce* today.

* * *

Begin your tour at the Visitor Center. There is an access road through the Visitor Center facility that connects the parking lots to the Baltimore Pike to the east and the Taneytown Road to the west. From any of the parking lots, drive west to the Taneytown Road.

As you reach the Taneytown Road, the small house to your right front on the other side of the road is the Leister House; this is where Meade established his headquarters.

Turn right on to the Taneytown Road and drive north for 0.5 mile to the intersection with Steinwehr Avenue (U.S. Business 15). The National Cemetery will be on your right as you drive on the Taneytown Road. At the intersection with Steinwehr Avenue, there is a stoplight. Steinwehr Avenue goes off to your right. Continue straight through the intersection and on to Washington Street. Drive on Washington Street for 0.6 mile to the intersection with Chambersburg Street. There is a stoplight at this intersection.

As you travel along Washington Street and out to Seminary Ridge and McPherson's Ridge, you will be following the route Brigadier General John Buford's cavalry division used as it went through Gettysburg on June 30. In 1863 the Eagle Hotel was on the northeast corner of the intersection of Washington Street and Chambersburg Street. This is where Buford established his headquarters.

Turn left on to Chambersburg Street, also named Highway U.S. 30 West. Drive west on this road. In 0.1 mile, at the stoplight, take the right fork and follow Highway 30. Continue to drive for another 0.9 mile. You will pass beyond the town and through a traffic light where Reynolds Avenue (a park road) intersects with Highway 30. At the first park road after the traffic light and just short of a small stone building, turn left and drive for 40 yards to a small parking area in the trees on your right behind the small stone building. Turn into the parking area and park. Leave your car and walk back to the Chambersburg Pike. Be extremely careful of traffic, and cross the highway. Walk to where the two statues are, stand between them, and face left (west). Gettysburg will be behind you as you are facing west.

Stop 1—Buford Delays and Reynolds Reinforces, July 1, 1863

You are standing on the western edge of McPherson's Ridge. The two statues are of Brigadier General John Buford and Major General John F. Reynolds. The Chambersburg Pike, also called the Cashtown Road, is to your left. In 1,100 yards the pike crosses Herr Ridge. Six miles west of where you are the pike passes by Cashtown. From there it continues over South Mountain to Chambersburg. Willoughby Run is in the low ground between you and Herr Ridge.

Herbst Wood is to your left and three-fourths of a mile farther left is the Hagerstown (Fairfield) Road. The barn to your left rear was part of the farm owned by the McPherson family in 1863. The house was in the lower ground on the other side of the barn. It burned in 1896. Beyond the barn at a greater distance to the east, where the white spire rises above the trees, you can see the Lutheran Seminary. Behind you (east) is Seminary Ridge. To your right rear on the other side of the railroad is Oak Ridge. One mile to your right (north) is Oak Hill. McPherson's, Seminary, and Oak Ridges are the key terrain controlling the avenues of advance and roads that approach Gettysburg from the west.

Buford's cavalry division established a position on McPherson's Ridge on the morning of July 1. You are in the right center of Colonel William Gamble's First Brigade. Gamble's position began to your right, on the other side of the railroad cut, and went south through where you are almost to the Hagerstown (Fairfield) Road. Colonel Thomas C. Devin's Second Brigade was deployed to Gamble's right and extended Buford's line to the Mummasburg Road, 1,200 yards (0.7 mile) to your right. Using outposts, Devin extended his line east of Seminary Ridge and north of Gettysburg. Four guns of Lieutenant John H. Calef's Battery A, Second U.S. Artillery, were deployed on either side of the Chambersburg Pike. Calef's other two guns were positioned on the other side of Herbst Woods.

In the early morning hours of July 1, Major General Henry Heth's division marched east on the Chambersburg Pike. Its first contact with Buford's troops was an outpost line on the other side of and along Herr Ridge. As Heth began to deploy, he placed Brigadier General Joseph R. Davis's brigade to the north of the pike and Brigadier General James J. Archer's brigade to the south. From Herr Ridge these two brigades moved forward against Buford's position. As the pressure built up on Buford's position, infantry reinforcement began to arrive. The first unit to arrive was Brigadier General Lysander Cutler's Second Brigade, First Division, First

Corps, which went into position to your right and left, occupying a position astride the Chambersburg Pike. Next to arrive was Brigadier General Solomon Meredith's Iron Brigade (First Brigade, First Division, First Corps). Meredith's brigade went into position to Cutler's left and in Herbst Woods. Captain James A. Hall deployed his Second Main Battery where you are. The cavalry withdrew and formed on the flanks of the infantry as additional First Corps infantry brigades continued to arrive.

Report of Brig. Gen. John Buford, USA, Commanding, First Cavalry Division, Cavalry Corps, Army of the Potomac

By daylight on July 1, I had gained positive information of the enemy's position and movements, and my arrangements were made for entertaining him until General Reynolds could reach the scene.

On July 1, between 8 and 9 A.M., reports came in from the First Brigade (Colonel Gamble's) that the enemy was coming down from toward Cashtown in force. Colonel Gamble made an admirable line of battle, and moved off proudly to meet him. The two lines soon became hotly engaged, we having the advantage of position, he of numbers. The First Brigade held its own for more than two hours, and had to be literally dragged back a few hundred yards to a position more secure and better sheltered. Tidball's battery [Battery A, Second U.S. Artillery], commanded by Lieutenant Calef, Second U.S. Artillery, fought on this occasion as is seldom witnessed. At one time the enemy had a concentric fire upon this battery from twelve guns, all at short range. Calef held his own gloriously, worked his guns deliberately with great judgment and skill, and with wonderful effect upon the enemy. The First Brigade maintained this unequal contest until the leading division of General Reynolds' corps came up to its assistance, and then most reluctantly did it give up the front. A portion of the Third Indiana found horse-holders, borrowed muskets, and fought with the Wisconsin regiment that came to relieve them. While this left of my line was engaged, Devin's brigade, on the right, had its hands full. The enemy advanced upon Devin by four roads, and on each was checked and held until the leading division of the Eleventh Corps came to his relief. [*OR*, vol. 27, pt. 1, 927]

Buford's delaying action, fought forward of and along this position, provided the time required for Reynolds to bring forward the First Corps infantry and artillery. Reynolds's decision committed the First Corps to decisive action along the low ridge where you are and behind you on Seminary and Oak Ridges. It also brought the Eleventh Corps into the fight north of Gettysburg, to your right rear. Lastly, it began the final series of decisions that brought all of the Army of the Potomac into a decisive battle at Gettysburg.

Return to your car for the drive to Stop 2. Be extremely careful of traffic as you walk across the Chambersburg Pike. Depart the parking lot, turn right, and follow Meredith Avenue through Herbst Woods for 0.4 mile where you will come to a T intersection with Reynolds Avenue. Turn left onto Reynolds Avenue, drive north for 50 yards, pull over to the right side of the road, and stop.

Look to your left, and you will see a small marker that shows where Reynolds was killed as he led troops forward into the wood.

Continue to drive north on Reynolds Avenue for 0.4 mile. You will cross the Chambersburg Pike and go over the railroad overpass to a T intersection. At the intersection turn left on to Buford Avenue. Follow Buford Avenue west and then north for 0.7 mile to the parking lot for the Eternal Light Peace Memorial. Park, get out of your car, and walk to the memorial. Go up on the terrace part of the memorial, and face so that you are looking south. You should be looking toward where you just came from.

Stop 2—Ewell and Rodes Decide to Attack Immediately on Arriving North of Gettysburg, July 1, 1863

You are on Oak Ridge, also known as Oak Hill at this location. As you look south, you can see at a distance of one mile the McPherson Barn and the area of Stop 1. The Confederate infantry and artillery that arrived in the vicinity of where you are was Major General Robert E. Rodes's division. Earlier Rodes had been north of this location and moving in a westerly direction toward Cashtown. When his corps commander, Lieutenant General Richard S. Ewell, received word from Lieutenant General Ambrose P. Hill that he was moving on Gettysburg, Rodes's Division was six miles north at Middletown (today's Biglerville). At the intersection of the east-west and north-south roads in Middletown, Rodes turned left. As his division marched south toward Gettysburg, he deployed his lead brigade. His division then moved off the road to the west, continued south on this wooded ridge, and deployed as it moved. When his division came out of the woods, it was centered where you are on Oak Ridge.

As Rodes came near the edge of the woods and looked south, as you are, this is what he saw: directly in front, at a distance, are the Chambersburg Pike, McPherson Barn, and Herbst Woods. In the woods and around the barn, Rodes saw the infantry and artillery of the First Corps, Army of the Potomac. Behind the barn, where the north-south park road is today, he saw the left of their battle line. Along the continuation of the park road north of the Chambersburg Pike and the railroad cut, marked by a bridge, was additional infantry. In the long tree line that begins 500 yards from your left front and goes south, he saw more Union troops. Farther to his left, in the lower open ground east of the ridge, he saw the infantry and artillery of the Eleventh Corps as they deployed.

Report of Maj. Gen. Robert E. Rodes, CSA, Commanding Rodes's Division, Ewell's Corps, Army of Northern Virginia

On July 1, in pursuance of the order to rejoin the army, the division resumed its march, but upon arriving at Middletown, and hearing that Lieutenant-General Hill's corps was moving upon Gettysburg, by order of General Ewell, the head of the column was turned in that direction: When within 4 miles of the town, to my surprise, the presence of the enemy there in force was announced by the sound of a sharp cannonade, and instant preparations for battle were made.

On arriving on the field, I found that by keeping along the wooded ridge, on the left side of which the town of Gettysburg is situated, I could strike the force of the enemy with which General Hill's troops were engaged upon the flank, and that, besides moving under cover, whenever we struck the enemy we could engage him with the advantage in ground. [*OR*, vol. 27, pt. 2, 552]

Rodes believed the First Corps right flank was in the northern edge of the tree line that is 500 yards to your left front. If you look closely to the left of the edge of the trees you will see a rock wall and monuments that go from south to north. Other Union forces were at that location. Because of the rock wall and the manner in which the ground falls off behind the wall, they could not be seen. Believing that he was in position to strike the right flank of the Union position facing west, which was the First Corps, Rodes ordered an attack.

Report of Maj. Gen. Robert E. Rodes, CSA—Continued

The division was, therefore, moved along the summit of the ridge, with only one brigade deployed at first, and finally, as the enemy's cavalry had discovered us and the ground was of such character as to admit of cover for a large opposing force, with three brigades deployed; Doles on the left, Rodes' (old) brigade, Colonel O'Neal commanding, in the center, and Iverson on the right, the artillery and the other two brigades moved up closely to the line of battle. The division had to move nearly a mile before coming in view of the enemy's forces, excepting a few mounted men, and finally arrived at a point—a prominent hill on the ridge—whence the whole of that portion of the force opposing General Hill's troops could be seen. To get at these troops properly, which were still over half a mile from us, it was necessary to move the whole of my command by the right flank, and to change direction to the right.

I determined to attack with my center and right, holding at bay still another force [elements of the Eleventh Corps], then emerging from the town (apparently with the intention of turning my left), with Doles' brigade, which was moved somewhat to the left for this purpose, and trusting to this gallant brigade thus holding them until General Early's division arrived, which I knew would be soon, and which would strike this portion of the enemy's force on the flank before it could overpower Doles.

At this moment Doles' brigade occupied the open plain between the Middletown [Carlisle] road and the foot of the ridge before spoken of. The Alabama [O'Neal's] brigade, with a wide interval between it and Doles', extended from this plain up the slope of the ridge [Iverson's brigade was on O'Neal's right]; Daniel's brigade supported Iverson's, and extended some distance to the right of it; Ramseur was in reserve. All the troops were in the woods excepting Doles' and a portion of Rodes [O'Neal's] brigades, but all were subjected to some loss or annoyance from the enemy's artillery.

I caused Iverson's brigade to advance, and at the same moment gave in person to O'Neal the order to attack, indicating to him precisely the point to which he was to direct the left of the four regiments then under his orders, the Fifth Alabama, which formed the extreme left of this brigade, being held in reserve, under my own immediate command, to defend the gap between O'Neal and Doles. Daniel was at the same moment instructed to advance to support Iverson, if necessary; if not, to attack on his right as soon as possible.

Carter's whole [artillery] battalion was by this time engaged hotly—a portion from the right, the remainder from the left of the hill—and was subjected to a heavy artillery fire in return. Iverson's brigade attacked handsomely, but suffered very heavily from the enemy's musketry fire from behind a stone wall along the crest of the ridge. The Alabama brigade went into action in some confusion, and with only three of its regiments (the Sixth, Twelfth, and Twenty-sixth), the Fifth having been retained by my order, and, for reasons explained to Colonel O'Neal, the Third having been permitted by Colonel O'Neal to move with Daniel's brigade.

In the meantime, General Early's division had been brought into action on my left with great success, and Doles, thus relieved, without waiting for orders, and though greatly outnumbered, boldly attacked the heavy masses of the enemy in his front. After a short but desperate contest, in which his brigade acted with unsurpassed gallantry, he succeeded in driving them before him, thus achieving on the left, and about the same time, a success no less brilliant than that of Ramseur, in the center, and Daniel, on the right. [*OR*, vol. 27, pt. 2, 552–54]

When Rodes attacked, he brought Early's Division, the remainder of Heth's Division, and Pender's Division into the fight. Contrary to Lee's instructions, by mid-afternoon almost one-half of his army had been decisively committed to a fight at Gettysburg. The result was the general engagement that Lee did not want until his army was concentrated. It's not that Lee was unwilling to fight at Gettysburg: he was prepared to fight the Army of the Potomac when he had his army concentrated. This concentration would not have occurred until the evening of July 1 or morning of July 2.

The next day (July 2), with all of his corps in close proximity to each other, Lee could have attacked or defended from a position of strength. The fighting on the first day created such heavy casualties in three of his divisions that they were of marginal strength for further offensive operations. This caused a piecemeal commitment of the remaining divisions as they arrived on the battlefield. This in turn prevented Lee from developing and deploying the full combat power of his army at a decisive point.

Return to your car for the drive to Stop 3.

Depart the parking lot by driving straight ahead. The Eternal Light Peace Memorial will be on your left. Follow the park road from the parking lot for 0.3 mile to a small steel observation tower and a small parking lot. You will cross the Mummasburg Road. Park and get out of your car. Walk up the tower, or stand at its base. Look to the southeast, toward Gettysburg.

Stop 3—Ewell Decides Not to Attack Cemetery Hill, July 1, 1863

The road behind you that you just crossed is the Mummasburg Road. To your right are a section of the rock wall and the monuments you saw from Stop 2. Where you are and to your right was the position of the Union troops that Rodes could not see. Farther to your right is the edge of the wood where Rodes thought the right flank of the First Corps was. To your left front across the lower open ground you can see a line of monuments that goes to the northeast. This line of monuments is continued on the other side of the Carlisle Road until it ends on Barlow's Knoll. The monuments mark the position of the Eleventh Corps. The corps' right flank was on the knoll.

Directly in front of you are Gettysburg College and the town of Gettysburg. Beyond the town and at a distance of 3,300 yards (1.9 miles) from your location, you can see the key terrain of Cemetery Hill and Culp's Hill. Cemetery Hill is on the right, Culp's Hill on the left.

During the afternoon fighting, Ewell was on Oak Ridge. From there he had the same general view of the high ground southeast of Gettysburg that you have. After the successful late afternoon attacks by Rodes's and Early's Divisions, Ewell rode across the open ground to your left and into Gettysburg. Ewell stopped at the town square. While at the square, he began to receive reports from his commanders. It was there that he received a report of a possible Union force to the east of Gettysburg. He also received Lee's order to "carry the hill [Cemetery Hill] if practicable, but avoid a general engagement." [*OR*, vol. 27, pt. 2, 318]

Ewell could not observe Cemetery Hill from the square so he traveled south on Baltimore Street to the edge of town where he could observe First and Eleventh Corps units going into defensive positions. Returning to the square, he received information that Hill would not be able to support him if he attacked. Sometime after that he made the decision not to attack Cemetery Hill.

Report of Lieut. Gen. Richard S. Ewell, CSA, Commanding, Ewell's Corps, Army of Northern Virginia

The enemy had fallen back to a commanding position known as Cemetery Hill, south of Gettysburg, and quickly showed a formidable front there. On entering the town, I received a message from the commanding general to attack this hill, if I could do so to advantage. I could not bring artillery to bear on it, and all the troops with me were jaded by twelve hours' marching and fighting, and I was notified that General Johnson's division (the only one of my corps that had not been engaged) was close to the town.

Cemetery Hill was not assailable from the town, and I determined, with Johnson's division, to take possession of a wooded hill [Culp's Hill] to my left, on a line with and commanding Cemetery Hill. Before Johnson got up, the enemy was reported moving to outflank our extreme left, and I could see what seemed to be his skirmishers in that direction.

Before this report could be investigated by Lieut. T. T. Turner, aide-de-camp of my staff, and Lieut. Robert D. Early, sent for that purpose, and Johnson placed in position, the night was far advanced. [*OR,* vol. 27, pt. 2, 445]

One of two outcomes may have occurred had Ewell attacked Cemetery Hill. First, if the attack were successful, then Meade's army would have been denied the key terrain on which it established its position at Gettysburg. A different position would have had to be established farther south, maybe at Emmitsburg or Pipe Creek. Possessing Cemetery Hill would have given Lee control of the roads going south and southeast out of Gettysburg. These roads could have facilitated the movement of his concentrated army toward the Army of the Potomac.

Second, if Ewell's attack proved unsuccessful, the continued deployment of his corps north of Cemetery Hill might have been abandoned, and Lee might have enforced his instructions for the corps to redeploy to Seminary Ridge. With all three of his corps positioned on Seminary Ridge, Lee's ability to deliver a powerful attack on the Union south flank would have been greatly increased. Instead of two divisions marching south to attack Meade's left flank on July 2, it could have been four.

Return to your car for the drive to Stop 4.

Leave the parking area, and drive south on Doubleday Avenue for 0.4 mile. Here the road makes a right turn. Drive for 0.1 mile to the intersection with Reynolds Avenue. You passed through this intersection on the way to Stop 2. Turn left on to Reynolds Avenue, and drive south for 0.2 mile to the intersection with the Chambersburg Pike. Turn left and drive east on the Chambersburg Pike for 0.2 mile to Seminary Ridge. The open field to your right just before you turn onto Seminary Ridge is where Lee's headquarters tents were from the night of July 1 until the end of the battle. Turn right on to Seminary Ridge, and drive south for 0.3 mile to Middle Street (the Hagerstown Road). The large building, with the cupola on top, to your left 0.1 mile after you make the turn, was the main Seminary building in 1863. At Middle Street (the Hagerstown Road), the road you are on becomes West Confederate Avenue. Cross Middle Street, and continue driving south for 0.8 mile to the North Carolina State Monument. Park on the right side of the road, get out of your car, and walk to the North Carolina State Monument. Take a position looking east so that West Confederate Avenue and the monument are behind you.

Stop 4—Lee Continues the Offensive, July 2, 1863

Lee and Longstreet met on the evening of July 1. This meeting took place close to the Lutheran Seminary's main building, where they could observe part of the Union position to their east on Cemetery Hill. During this meeting Lee informed Longstreet that he planned to continue offensive operations the next day. Longstreet disagreed with the decision, but he was overruled and departed to bring his corps forward.

Although Lee had decided to continue on the offense, he had not developed an exact plan of attack. During the night and early the next morning, he discussed with Ewell the possibility of conducting the main attack against Culp's Hill and/or Cemetery Hill but soon discarded this option.

Early on the morning of July 2, part of Lee's staff conducted a reconnaissance of the area to the south, and he also did some reconnaissance on his own. Lee rode along Seminary Ridge so that he could observe as much of the Union position as possible. This probably brought him south from his headquarters to this vicinity. He could not have safely gone farther south. Major General Richard H. Anderson's division was going into position and was fighting with Union patrols and skirmishers.

From this position you can see what Lee saw. The Emmitsburg Road is directly in front of you at a distance of 1,200 yards (0.7 mile). An additional 260 yards beyond the Emmitsburg Road is the "Copse of Trees" that played a predominant role on July 3. The high ground to the left of the trees is Cemetery Hill. Beyond that, but not observable, is Culp's Hill. Meade's defensive line began on Culp's Hill and came west to Cemetery Hill. There, where it could be seen from this location, the line of deployed Union troops turned south and went along Cemetery Ridge. It went past the Copse of Trees, then to your right past where the tall spire-like monument is today, and on toward and past the large monument with the dome on top (the Pennsylvania State Monument). There Lee would have lost view of this line of troops. However, he could see along the Emmitsburg Road, from about where the red barn marks the Codori farm, a line of troops going south to where you see a small white building. This white building is next to the Klingle house. This line of troops consisted of skirmishers and was not the main line; the line appeared to end at the Klingle house because the ground drops away and is out of view. Lee believed Meade's left flank ended near or east of the Klingle house. To the left and farther on from the white building, you can see Little Round Top and Big Round Top. Lee did not yet have information about these two prominent terrain features, and the information he later received was incorrect.

After gathering as much information as possible, Lee decide to march Longstreet's two divisions south behind Seminary Ridge, form them on what he believed to be the south flank of Meade's position, and have them attack along the Emmitsburg Road. As they attacked from your right to left, Anderson's Division was to join them. Ewell was ordered to conduct a demonstration against Cemetery Hill and Culp's Hill when he heard Longstreet's attack begin. If the situation proved favorable, Ewell was given the discretion to convert the demonstration into an attack.

Report of Gen. Robert E. Lee, CSA, Commanding Army of Northern Virginia

It had not been intended to deliver a general battle so far from our base unless attacked, but coming unexpectedly upon the whole Federal Army, to withdraw through the mountains with our extensive trains would have been difficult and dangerous. At the same time we were unable to await an attack, as the country was unfavorable for collecting supplies in the presence of the enemy, who could restrain our foraging parties by holding the mountain passes with local and other troops. A battle had, therefore, become in a measure unavoidable, and the success already gained gave hope of a favorable issue.

The enemy occupied a strong position, with his right upon two commanding elevations adjacent to each other, one [Culp's Hill] southeast and the other, known as Cemetery Hill, immediately south of the town, which lay at its base. His line extended thence upon the high ground along the Emmitsburg road, with a steep ridge in rear, which was also occupied. This ridge was difficult of ascent, particularly the two hills above mentioned as forming its northern extremity, and a third at the other end [Little Round Top], on which the enemy's left rested. Numerous stone and rail fences along the slope served to afford protection to his troops and impede our advance. In his front, the ground was undulating and generally open for about three-quarters of a mile.

General Ewell's corps constituted our left, Johnson's division being opposite the height adjoining Cemetery Hill, Early's in the center, in front of the north face of the latter, and Rodes upon his right. Hill's corps faced the west side of Cemetery Hill, and extended nearly parallel to the Emmitsburg road, making an angle with Ewell's, Pender's division formed his left, Anderson's his right, Heth's, under Brigadier-General Pettigrew, being in reserve. His artillery, under Colonel [R. Lindsay] Walker, was posted in eligible positions along his line.

It was determined to make the principal attack upon the enemy's left, and endeavor to gain a position from which it was thought that our artillery could be brought to bear with effect. Longstreet was directed to place the divisions of McLaws and Hood on the right of Hill, partially enveloping the enemy's left, which he was to drive in.

General Hill was ordered to threaten the enemy's center, to prevent re-enforcements being drawn to either wing, and co-operate with his right division in Longstreet's attack.

General Ewell was instructed to make a simultaneous demonstration upon the enemy's right, to be converted into a real attack should opportunity offer. [*OR,* vol. 27, pt. 2, 318–19]

His plan completed, Lee issued Longstreet his orders about 10:00 A.M. After the complete arrival of his two divisions, Longstreet began his march to the south about noon.

Return to your car for the drive to Stop 5.

Continue driving south on West Confederate Avenue for 0.3 mile to the Virginia State Monument. Park in the parking area or along the right side of the road, leave your car, and walk east along the walking path, going away from the monument, for 250 yards to a rise in the ground.

Stop 5—Lee Attacks the Union Center, July 3, 1863

Directly in front of you, 1,100 yards away, is the Copse of Trees and "The Angle." These were the right center of the objective for the attack on July 3. Slightly to the right along the Emmitsburg Road and 900 yards from where you are is the red Codori barn. Look to your right, and you will see the Spangler House 650 yards from your location. Beyond the Spangler House is the Sherfy House. Beyond the Sherfy House and just across the Emmitsburg Road is the Peach Orchard. The Peach Orchard is 1,400 yards (0.8 mile) from your location.

Beginning at the Peach Orchard, the artillery line of Longstreet's Corps came in your direction. Longstreet had sixty-five guns deployed from the Peach Orchard northward for 1,350 yards, just to your right. Pickett's Division formed for the attack in the low ground and woods to your right rear.

Sixty-eight guns from Hill's Corps were deployed behind you and to your left, along West Confederate Avenue. To your left rear, Brigadier General J. Johnston Pettigrew and Major General Isaac R. Trimble formed their units for the attack.

The artillery on either side of you commenced firing just after 1:00 P.M. This cannonade continued until just before 3:00 P.M. At that time the order was given for the infantry attack. From the woods to your left and the low ground to your right, approximately 12,000 Confederate infantry marched toward the center of Meade's position.

Report of Gen. Robert E. Lee, CSA—Continued

The result of this day's [July 2] operations induced the belief that, with proper concert of action, and with the increased support that the positions gained on the right would enable the artillery to render the assaulting columns, we should ultimately succeed, and it was accordingly determined to continue the attack.

A careful examination was made of the ground secured by Longstreet, and his batteries placed in positions, which, it was believed, would enable them to silence those of the enemy. Hill's artillery and part of Ewell's was ordered to open simultaneously, and the assaulting column to advance under cover of the combined fire of the three. The batteries were directed to be pushed forward as the infantry progressed, protect their flanks, and support their attacks closely.

About 1 P.M., at a given signal, a heavy cannonade was opened, and continued for about two hours with marked effect upon the enemy. His batteries replied vigorously at first, but toward the close their fire slackened perceptibly, and General Longstreet ordered forward the column of attack, consisting of Pickett's and Heth's divisions, in two lines, Pickett on the right. Wilcox's brigade marched in rear of Pickett's right, to guard that flank, and Heth's was supported by Lane's and Scales' brigades [of Pender's Division], under General Trimble.

The troops moved steadily on, under a heavy fire of musketry and artillery, the main attack being directed against the enemy's left center.

His batteries reopened as soon as they appeared. Our own having nearly exhausted their ammunition in the protracted cannonade that preceded the advance of the infantry, were unable to reply, or render the necessary support to the attacking party. Owing to this fact, which was unknown to me when the assault took place, the enemy was enabled to throw a strong force of infantry against our left, already wavering under a concentrated fire of artillery from the ridge in front, and from Cemetery Hill, on the left. It finally gave way, and the right, after penetrating the enemy's lines, entering his advance works, and capturing some of his artillery, was attacked simultaneously in front and on both flanks, and driven back with heavy loss. [*OR*, vol. 27, pt. 2, 320–21]

Lee made his decision to attack in the center as he moved to various locations. Initially he was at the Peach Orchard. There Longstreet informed him he could not carry out the original plan for Hood's, McLaws's, and Pickett's Divisions to continue the July 2 attack. From the Peach Orchard he would have come back toward this location along ground that allowed him to study Meade's defenses. Lee then decided to attack Meade's center. He probably issued the attack order to Longstreet on the ground to your right. Lee observed the attack from this vicinity.

Return to your car for the drive to Stop 6.

Continue driving south on West Confederate Avenue for 0.9 mile to the intersection with the Millerstown Road. At the intersection of West Confederate Avenue and Millerstown Road, turn right and drive west for 0.5 mile to the intersection with Black Horse Tavern Road. Turn right on to Black Horse Tavern Road and drive north 1.3 miles to a raised piece of ground. Be careful of traffic in both directions. Do a U-turn and park alongside the road so that you are looking back to where you just came from. *Be sure to park so that you can be seen by traffic coming from both directions.*

Stop 6—Longstreet Orders the Countermarch, July 2, 1863

Black Horse Tavern Road intersects with the Hagerstown Road 0.5 mile behind you. Black Horse Tavern was at the northeast section of this intersection. Black Horse Tavern Road continues on from there in a north and northwest direction. Major General Lafayette McLaws's and Major General John B. Hood's divisions began their march toward the Union left on Black Horse Tavern Road from the other side of the intersection. With Brigadier General Joseph Kershaw's brigade of McLaws's Division leading, they marched in this direction. McLaws was riding a little ahead of his division. When he came up on this piece of ground, he stopped the march. Longstreet then came forward to find out why the column was halted. Look directly ahead, and at a distance of 3,900 yards (2.2 miles) you will see Big Round Top. To the left of Big Round Top is Little Round Top. Today you cannot see it because of the height of the trees along Seminary Ridge. However, in 1863 Little Round Top was visible from this location. Conversely, this location could also be seen from there. Longstreet and McLaws saw the flags of the Union signal station there and knew if they continued on this route, they would be seen and their movement reported. Meade's receipt of this information would remove the element of surprise from Lee's plan and provide him time to redeploy units.

Narrative of Maj. Gen. Lafayette McLaws, CSA, Commanding McLaws's Division, Longstreet's Corps, Army of Northern Virginia

Suddenly, as we rose a hill on the road we were taking, the [Little] Round Top was plainly visible, with the flags of the signal men in rapid motion. I sent back and halted my division and rode with [Captain] Johnston rapidly around the neighborhood to see if there was any road by which we could go into position without being seen. Not finding any I joined my command and met General Longstreet there, who asked, "What is the matter?" I replied, "Ride with me and I will show you that we can't go on this route, according to instructions, without being seen by the enemy." We rode to the top of the hill and he at once said, "Why this won't do. Is there no way to avoid it?" I then told him of my reconnaissance in the morning, and he said: "How can we get there?" I said: "Only by going back—by countermarching." He said: "Then all right," and the movement commenced. But as General Hood, in his eagerness for the fray (and he bears the character of always being so), had pressed on his division behind mine so that it lapped considerably, creating confusion in the countermarch, General Longstreet rode to me and said: "General, there is so much confusion, owing to Hood's division being mixed up with yours, suppose you let him countermarch first and lead in the attack." I replied: "General, as I started in the lead, let me continue so;" and he replied, "Then go on," and rode off. [McLaws, "Gettysburg," *SHSP,* vol. 7, 69]

It was at this location that Longstreet ordered the column to reverse its direction of march and move to a location where it could march in low ground and continue south. The reversal was done by having the head of the column double back. This produced a traffic jam on the road that slowed all movement. North of the Hagerstown Road, a route was found that allowed Longstreet's force to march in the low ground between you and Seminary Ridge.

Colonel E. Porter Alexander had also passed this way with his artillery battalion. When he came to this location, rather than turn around, he went off to your right, moved around the higher ground, and regained the road farther on.

You will now follow beside and then on the route of McLaws's Division after it completed the countermarch and moved into lower ground. This will take you back to the intersection of the Millerstown Road and West Confederate Avenue.

Drive south on Black Horse Tavern Road for 1.3 miles to the intersection with the Millerstown Road. After you have driven 0.9 mile, you will cross Willoughby Run. McLaws's Division rejoined the road at this point.

At the intersection of Black Horse Tavern Road and Millerstown Road, turn left and drive east for 0.1 mile, pull off to the side of the road, and stop.

Stop 7—"How Are You Going In?" July 2, 1863

Along this part of the route McLaws and Longstreet had a conversation as to how McLaws's Division would deploy. To Longstreet's question, "How are you going in?" McLaws replied, "That will be determined when I can see what is in my front." Longstreet then said, "There is nothing to your front; you will be entirely on the flank of the enemy." McLaws then told Longstreet, "Then I will continue on my march in column of companies, and after arriving on the flank, as far as necessary will face to the left and march on the enemy." Satisfied with this answer, Longstreet rode away and McLaws's Division, led by Brigadier General Joseph B. Kershaw's brigade continued along the road [McLaws, "Gettysburg," *SHSP,* vol. 7, 69–70].

The tall tower you see in front of you is on West Confederate Avenue. It is at your next stop. Continue driving for 0.4 mile to the intersection of Millerstown Road with West Confederate Avenue. Turn right onto West Confederate Avenue and drive 0.1 mile; then turn left into the parking area at the base of the steel tower. Park, get out of your car, walk east past the tower, and through the thin tree line. Stand 20 yards in front of the tower with the thin tree line behind you, so that you have a view of the open fields, the Emmitsburg Road, and the Peach Orchard.

Stop 8—Not as Planned, July 2, 1863

As you look east across the fields, the terrain appears much as it did in 1863. Going from your left to right, north to south, is the Emmitsburg Road. Directly in front of you on the other side of the Emmitsburg Road is the Peach Orchard. The Wentz home was in the northern part of the orchard, and only a foundation remains today. To your left is the Millerstown Road and the Warfield House; both were there in 1863. Farther to your left, alongside the road, you can see the houses and barns of the Sherfy, Klingle, and Codori farms. They look much today as they did at the time of the battle. Lee thought Meade's left, or south, flank was in the vicinity or slightly south of the Klingle home. To your right front you can see Little Round Top and Big Round Top. Between them and you, but hidden by the trees in the distance, is Devil's Den. On the other side of the trees to the right of and beyond the Peach Orchard is the Wheatfield.

The plan was for McLaws's Division to continue marching on the Millerstown Road, onto and past the Emmitsburg Road. There the companies would left wheel into a battle line and attack what was believed to be Meade's left flank. However, as Kershaw approached the crest of Seminary Ridge, he was confronted by part of Sickles's Third Corps and was forced to deploy along the ridge. Kershaw deployed to your right and the next brigade, Brigadier General William Barksdale's, deployed to your left on the other side of the road. Brigadier General Paul J. Semmes deployed his brigade in a supporting position behind Kershaw while Brigadier General William T. Wofford did the same behind Barksdale. Colonel Alexander's artillery battalion deployed where you are and to your left. Colonel Cabell's artillery battalion deployed farther to your right.

As the Confederate commanders looked east, they saw a Union position of infantry and artillery that began along the Emmitsburg Road 1,500 yards to your left front, just on the other side of the Klingle house. From there it came south to the Peach Orchard, where it turned east and went to the Wheatfield, and then turned south and went to Devil's Den.

Report of Brig. Gen. Joseph B. Kershaw, CSA, Commanding Kershaw's Brigade, McLaws's Division, Longstreet's Corps, Army of Northern Virginia

Arriving at the school-house, on the road leading across the Emmitsburg road by the peach orchard, then in possession of the enemy, the lieutenant-general commanding [Longstreet] directed me to advance my brigade and attack the enemy at that point, turn his flank, and extend along the cross-road, with my left resting toward the Emmitsburg road. At the same time a battery of artillery was moved along the road parallel with my line of march. About 3 P.M. the head of my column came into the open field in front of a stone wall, and in view of the enemy. I immediately filed to the right along and in front of the wall, and formed line of battle under cover of my skirmishers, then engaged with those of the enemy, these extending along the Emmitsburg road.

In the meantime, examining the position of the enemy, I found him to be in superior force in the orchard, supported by artillery, with a main line of battle intrenched in the rear and extending to and upon the rocky mountain [Little Round Top] to his left far beyond the point at which his flank had supposed to rest. To carry out my instructions, would have been, if successful in driving him from the orchard, to present my own right and rear to a large portion of his line of battle. I therefore communicated the position of things to the major-general commanding [McLaws], and placed my line in position under cover of the stone wall. Along this wall the division was then formed, Semmes in reserve to me and Barksdale on my left, supported by Wofford, in reserve. Artillery [Cabell's Battalion] was also placed along the wall to my right, and Colonel De Saussure's Fifteenth South Carolina Regiment was thrown beyond it to protect it. Hood's division was then moving in our rear toward our right, to gain the enemy's left flank, and I was directed to commence the attack so soon as General Hood became engaged, swinging around toward the peach orchard, and at the same time establishing connection with Hood, on my right, and co-operating with him. It was understood he was to sweep down the enemy's line in a direction perpendicular to our then line of battle. I was told that Barksdale would move with me and conform to my movement. [*OR*, vol. 27, pt. 2, 367]

The presence of Union troops in that location was totally unexpected and required Longstreet to make a major modification to Lee's plan.

Narrative of Maj. Gen. Lafayette McLaws, CSA —Continued

My head of column soon reached the edge of the woods, and the enemy at once opened on it with numerous artillery, and one rapid glance showed them to be in force much greater than I had, and extending considerably beyond my right. My command, therefore, instead of marching on as directed, by head of column, deployed at once. Kershaw, a very cool, judicious and gallant gentleman, immediately turned the head of his column and marched by flank to right, and put his men under cover of a stone wall. Barksdale, the fiery, impetuous Mississippian, following, came into line on the left of Kershaw, his men sheltered by trees and part of a stone wall and under a gentle declivity. Besides the artillery firing, the enemy were advancing a strong line of skirmishers and threatening an advance in line. I hurried back to quicken the march of those in rear, and sent orders for my artillery to move to my right and open fire, so as to draw the fire of the opposite artillery from my infantry.

While this was going on I rode forward, and getting off my horse, went to some trees in advance and took a good look at the situation, and the view presented astonished me, as the enemy was massed in my front, and extended to my right and left as far as I could see.

The firing on my command showed to Hood in my rear that the enemy was in force in my front and right, and the head of his column was turned by General Longstreet's order to go on my right and as his troops appeared, the enemy opened on them, developing a long line to his right even, and way up to the top of [Little] Round Top. Thus was presented a state of affairs which was certainly not contemplated when the original plan or order of battle was given, and certainly was not known to General Longstreet a half hour previous.

Hood had been in the meanwhile moving towards the enemy's left, but he never did go far enough to envelop the left, not even partially. The charge of my division was ordered. General Kershaw, with his South Carolina brigade, leading, followed by Semmes with his Georgia brigade; then Barksdale, and Wofford last. [McLaws, "Gettysburg," *SHSP*, vol. 7, 70–71, 73]

Return to your car for the drive to Stop 9.

Drive south on West Confederate Avenue for 0.5 mile to the Emmitsburg Road. Turn left on to the Emmitsburg Road, and drive north for 0.7 mile to the Peach Orchard. At the Peach Orchard, turn right onto Wheatfield Road, drive 0.1 mile to the small parking area on the right side of the road, and park. Get out of your car and walk back west beside the road for 90 yards to the highest point of ground where you can look west across the Emmitsburg Road to Stop 8 and beyond.

Stop 9—Sickles Moves Forward to the Peach Orchard, July 2, 1863

In 1863 the Peach Orchard was on both sides of the Wheatfield Road. At 4:00 P.M. on July 2, this was part of Major General Daniel E. Sickles's Third Corps position. You are standing in the right center of Major General David B. Birney's First Division of the Third Corps. Brigadier General Charles K. Graham's First Brigade was deployed where you are and to your right for approximately 400 yards. Birney's two other brigades, Colonel P. Regis De Trobriand's and Brigadier General J. H. Hobart Ward's, were deployed in the Wheatfield and toward Devil's Den. To the right of Graham's brigade was Brigadier General Andrew A. Humphreys's Second Division. Humphreys had two brigades deployed along the Emmitsburg Road. Colonel William R. Brewster's Second Brigade was to Graham's immediate right. To Burling's right was Brigadier General Joseph B. Carr's First Brigade. Colonel George C. Burling's Third Brigade was in reserve.

Report of Maj. Gen. David B. Birney, USA, Commanding First Division, Third Corps, Army of the Potomac

At 7 A.M., under orders from Major-General Sickles, I relieved Geary's division, and formed a line, resting its left on the Sugar Loaf Mountain [Little Round Top] and the right thrown in a direct line toward the cemetery, connecting on the right with the Second Division of this corps. My picket line was in the Emmitsburg road, with sharpshooters some 300 yards in advance.

At 12 m. [noon], believing from the constant fire of the enemy that a movement was being made toward the left, I received permission from Major-General Sickles to send 100 of Berdan's [First U.S.] Sharpshooters, with the Third Maine Regiment as a support, and feel the enemy's right. The force sent by me was driven back by overwhelming numbers, with the loss of about 60, killed and wounded.

Communicating this important information to Major-General Sickles, I was ordered by that officer to change my front to meet the attack. I did this by advancing my left 500 yards [to Houck's Ridge and Devil's Den], and swinging around the right so as to rest on the Emmitsburg road at the peach orchard.

My line was formed with Ward on the left, resting on [Houck's Ridge], De Trobriand in the center [in the Wheatfield], and Graham on my right in the peach orchard, with his right [along] the Emmitsburg road. Smith's battery of rifled guns was placed [above Devil's Den] so as to command the gorge at the base of the Sugar Loaf Mountain [Little Round Top]; Winslow's battery on the right of Ward's brigade, and a battery from the Artillery Reserve; also Clark's and Ames' batteries to the right, in rear of the peach orchard, supported by Graham's brigade, and the Third

Michigan, from the Third Brigade, and the Third Maine, from the Second Brigade. Randolph's, Seeley's, and Turnbull's batteries were placed near the Emmitsburg road, on the front, parallel with it.

At 4 o'clock the enemy returned the artillery fire on my entire front, and advanced their infantry *en masse,* covered by a cloud of skirmishers. [*OR,* vol. 27, pt. 1, 482–83]

Report of Brig. Gen. Andrew A. Humphreys, USA, Commanding Second Division, Third Corps, Army of the Potomac

At an early hour of the morning, my division was massed in the vicinity of its bivouac, facing the Emmitsburg road, near the crest of the ridge [Cemetery Ridge] running from the cemetery of Gettysburg, in a southerly direction, to a rugged, conical-shaped hill, which I find goes by the name of Round Top, about 2 miles from Gettysburg.

Shortly after midday, I was ordered to form my division in line of battle, my left joining the right of the First Division of the Third Corps, Major-General Birney commanding, and my right resting opposite the left of General Caldwell's division, of the Second Corps, which was massed on the crest near my place of bivouac. The line I was directed to occupy was near the foot of the westerly slope of the ridge I have already mentioned, from which the ground rose to the Emmitsburg road, which runs on the crest of a ridge nearly parallel to the Round Top [Cemetery] ridge. This second ridge declines again immediately west of the road, at the distance of [550] yards from which the edge of a wood runs parallel to it. This wood was occupied by the enemy, whose pickets [Richard H. Anderson's] were exchanging shots from an early hour in the morning with our pickets thrown out beyond the road on the westerly slope.

About 4 P.M., in compliance with General Sickles' orders, I moved my division forward, so that the first line ran along the Emmitsburg road a short distance behind the crest upon which that road lies. As the division moved forward in two lines, as heretofore described, the enemy opened with artillery, which enfiladed us from the left, and subsequently with artillery on our front, both with but little effect. In reply to my inquiry whether I should attack, I was directed to remain in position. [*OR,* vol. 27, pt. 1, 531–32]

When the two divisions advanced to these positions, Sickles's right flank was exposed and 900 yards forward of the Second Corps left flank. His left flank in Devil's Den was also exposed, and Little Round Top was undefended.

The question is this: why were they here?

Turn around and face to the east, the direction you were driving, so that you can look down Wheatfield Road.

Look to your left and right, and you will see that you are standing on a slightly elevated plateau. The plateau is 450 yards wide north to south, or from your left to your right. It is 350 yards at its maximum to 140 yards deep, east to west. It has width and depth and is flat. This made it an ideal position for Civil War artillery. As you look east down the Wheatfield Road, you can see how the ground drops away. There is a thirty- to forty-foot difference in elevation between this plateau and where the center of Sickles's position initially was.

The initial position of Sickles's Corps was on the left of the Second Corps. From there his corps line went south along Cemetery Ridge into the low ground 1,400 yards (0.8 mile) in front of you and then up on Little Round Top. Remembering his experience at Chancellorsville when Confederate infantry and artillery occupied the key terrain at Hazel Grove, Sickles decided to move forward to this location to deny it to Lee's infantry and artillery. Although it placed his corps in an unsupported position, it presented Longstreet and McLaws with a totally unexpected tactical situation.

When Longstreet arrived on the southern part of Seminary Ridge, he expected to find the Union flank to his left, somewhere along or east of the Emmitsburg Road. Meade's left flank had never been in that location. Had Sickles not moved forward, Longstreet would have had several options. He could have continued to move forward, deploying McLaws's Division as it reached the area of the Rose Farm (to your right) and the Wheatfield (behind the trees in front of you). Hood's Division might have deployed to the right of McLaws's or followed in a supporting role, thereby adding depth to the attack. Deploying to the right would have resulted in Hood advancing through Devil's Den, then making contact with the left of the Sickles's line as he approached Little Round Top. This deployment would have given Longstreet a more compact battle line and offered the possibility of flanking Little Round Top on the south as the attack progressed east. It would also have given Sickles a shorter defensive position that would have been easier to reinforce.

Another option would have been for Hood's Division to deploy behind McLaws's Division, using it to protect his flank, and with Major General Richard H. Anderson's division joining in the attack, to advance northeast (as Lee had initially intended) and strike the Union position. This option could have exposed Longstreet's attack to a flanking counterattack by the Third and/or Fifth Corps.

However, this was not the situation confronting Longstreet. In front of him was a Union position that went to his left and right. Faced with this situation, he was forced into the time-consuming activity of deploying one division at the same time he was trying to find the Union flank, moving his other division to the right and deploying it into a battle line. These actions again used up more of the remaining time available for the attack.

Sickles's move forward had set the character of the fighting on the south flank. Everything that followed flowed from that decision.

Return to your car for the drive to Stop 10.

Drive forward a short distance to the intersection with a park road from the left, then do a U-turn, and drive back to the Emmitsburg Road. Turn left on to the Emmitsburg Road, and drive south for 0.7 mile to the intersection with South Confederate Avenue. Turn left onto South Confederate Avenue, and drive for 120 yards to the Texas State Monument. It is a monolithic red granite monument on the right side of the road. Park on the side of the road, get out of your car, and walk left to the other side of the road. The Texas Monument and the road are now behind you.

Stop 10—Longstreet Attacks the Union Left, July 2, 1863

With your back to the road, as you look east, Big Round Top is 1,400 yards (0.8 mile) in front of you. Little Round Top is slightly to the left of Big Round Top and 1,600 yards (0.9 mile) from your location. Between you and Little Round Top, at a distance of 1,100 yards (0.6 mile), is Devil's Den. Devil's Den was the left flank of Meade's defense; no one was on Little Round Top, yet. The Peach Orchard is 1,400 yards (0.8 mile) to your left.

You are at the location where Major General John B. Hood deployed his division late on Thursday afternoon. Hood's Division was following McLaws's as it turned off the Black Horse Tavern Road onto Millerstown Road. When McLaws's Division made contact with Sickles's position at the Peach Orchard, Hood moved to the right of the intended route and marched south to this location. Brigadier General Jerome B. Robertson's brigade deployed where you are. The Arkansas State Monument on the other side of the Emmitsburg Road marks its left flank. Brigadier General Evander M. Law's brigade deployed to the right of Robertson's. Brigadier General George T. Anderson deployed his brigade in a supporting position behind Robertson's Brigade while Brigadier General Henry L. Benning deployed behind Law's Brigade.

By the time this was done, it was late in the afternoon, sometime around 4:00 P.M. However, Longstreet had followed through on Lee's intent. When faced with an unexpected tactical situation in the area of the Peach Orchard, he had modified the plan and placed part of his corps on the left flank of Meade's defenses.

While preparing to attack, Hood received information on which he proposed to Longstreet that he move his division farther east and then attack.

Letter of Maj. Gen. John B. Hood, CSA, Commanding Hood's Division, Longstreet's Corps, Army of Northern Virginia, to Lieut. Gen. James Longstreet, CSA

The instructions I received were to place my division across the Emmetsburg road, form line of battle, and attack. Before reaching this road, however, I had sent forward some of my picked Texas scouts to ascertain the position of the enemy's extreme left flank. They soon reported to me that it rested upon Round Top mountain; that the country was open and that I could march through an open woodland pasture around Round Top and assault the enemy in flank and rear; that their wagon trains were parked in rear of their line, and were badly exposed to our attack in that direction. As soon as I arrived upon the Emmetsburg road I placed one or two batteries in position and opened fire. A reply from the enemy's guns soon developed his lines. His left rested on or near Round Top, with line bending back and again forward, forming, as it were, a concave line as approached by the Emmetsburg road. A considerable body of troops was posted in front of their main line, between the Emmetsburg road and Round Top mountain. This force was in line of battle upon an eminence near a peach orchard.

I found that in making the attack according to orders, viz: up the Emmetsburg road, I should have first to encounter and drive off this advanced line of battle; secondly, at the base and along the slope of the mountain, to confront immense boulders of stone, so massed together as to form narrow openings, which would break our ranks and cause the men to scatter whilst climbing up the rocky precipice. I found, moreover, that my division would be exposed to a heavy fire from the main line of the enemy, in position on the crest of the high range, of which Round Top was the extreme left, and, by reason of the concavity of the enemy's main line, that we would be subject to a destructive fire in flank and rear, as well as in front; and deemed it almost an impossibility to clamber along the boulders up this steep and rugged mountain, and, under this number of crossfires, put the enemy to flight. I knew that if the feat was accomplished it must be at a most fearful sacrifice of as brave and gallant soldiers as ever engaged in battle.

The reconnaissance by my Texas scouts and the development of the Federal lines were effected in a very short space of time; in truth, shorter than I have taken to recall and jot down these facts, although the scenes and events of that day are as clear to my mind as if the great battle had been fought yesterday. I was in possession of these important facts so shortly after reaching the Emmetsburg road, that I considered it my duty to report to you [Longstreet] at once my opinion, that it was unwise to attack up the Emmetsburg road, as ordered, and to urge that you allow me to turn Round Top and attack the enemy in flank and rear. Accordingly, I dispatched a staff officer bearing to you my request to be allowed to make the proposed movement on account of the above stated reasons. Your reply was quickly received: "General Lee's orders are to attack up the Emmetsburg road." I sent another officer to say that I feared nothing could be accomplished by such an attack, and renewed my request to turn Round Top. Again your answer was: "General Lee's orders are to attack up the Emmetsburg road." During this interim I had continued the use of the batteries upon the enemy, and had become more and more convinced that the Federal line extended to Round Top, and that I could not reasonably hope to accomplish much by the attack as ordered.

A third time I dispatched one of my staff to explain fully in regard to the situation, and to suggest that you had better come and look for yourself. I selected, in this instance, my adjutant general, Colonel Harry Sellers, whom you know to be not only an officer of great courage, but also of marked ability. Colonel Sellers returned with the same message: "General Lee's orders are to attack up the Emmetsburg road." Almost simultaneously, [Major] Fairfax, of your staff, rode up and repeated the above orders. [Fairfax was followed by Longstreet, who also came to Hood's location.]

> After this urgent protest against entering into battle at Gettysburg according to instructions—which protest is the first and only one I ever made during my entire military career—I ordered my line to advance and make the assault. [Letter from Hood to Longstreet, *SHSP,* vol. 4, 148–50]

The redeployment proposed by Hood would have positioned his division in the vicinity of the Taneytown Road, 2,300 yards (1.3 miles) directly east of your location. This would give him the capability of outflanking both Big and Little Round Top. The question was how to get there. The fastest way would have been to go south on the Emmitsburg Road for 0.7 mile, where it meets a road that goes southeast. In 0.5 mile that road intersects with a road that goes northeast for 1.2 miles and intersects with the Taneytown Road. The total distance is 2.4 miles. The time for the lead element to move this distance would have been about one hour after the march began. Add another hour to one and one-half hours for the trail units to complete the march and then at least another thirty minutes to an hour until the division was totally deployed for attack, and there is a lapse time of two and one-half to three hours before Hood could attack. Hood could also have marched his division cross-country to the Taneytown Road. While the distance was shorter, that route's elevated terrain and woods would have slowed the march, and thus the arrival time would have been about the same. At best Hood's attack would have begun around 6:30 or 7:00 P.M. Sunset on July 2, 1863 was at 7:41 P.M., and it was dark in another thirty minutes.

In addition, Hood's Division was no longer out of sight of the Union defenders. The artillery positioned where you are was part of Major Mathias W. Henry's battalion and was dueling with the artillery at the Peach Orchard. Brigadier General Gouverneur K. Warren on Little Round Top had already sent out a request for troops to come to that location. In another hour or two the entire defensive situation on Meade's left would have been different.

The question of time had to be a major factor in weighing the options. Longstreet's two divisions had taken longer than planned to move into the positions where they were now. More time would be required to redeploy Hood's Division farther east. This delay might have meant that there would not be enough time to conduct the attack that day. A postponement of the attack until the next day could allow the addition of Major General George Pickett's division. However, it would also give Meade the night of July 2–3 and perhaps even the early morning hours of July 3 to reposition additional forces to his left flank.

The loss of the element of surprise, the unexpected positions of Sickles's Third Corps, the loss of time in conducting the countermarch, the rapidly approaching night, and a lack of additional forces all contributed to limiting Longstreet's courses of action. He decided that his corps must attack from the positions now occupied by his two divisions. McLaws's Division attacked the Union positions centered on the Peach Orchard and the ground to the east. Hood's Division went for Devil's Den and Little Round Top.

The meeting between Hood and Longstreet was about where you are. Shortly after the attack began, Hood was wounded just in front of you.

Return to your car for the drive to Stop 11.

Continue driving forward on South Confederate Avenue for 0.2 mile to the Alabama State Monument. It is on your right. Park on the side of the road, get out of your car, and face left. You should be looking at Big Round Top.

Stop 11—Law Goes for the Artillery, and Benning Follows the Wrong Attack, July 2, 1863

Big Round Top is 1,400 yards (0.8 mile) in front of you. Little Round Top is just to the left of Big Round Top and 1,600 yards (0.9 mile) from your location. Devils' Den—the location of the Union left flank—is 1,100 yards (0.6 mile) to your left front. The Taneytown Road, 500 yards from Little Round Top, was one of Meade's supply and communication routes. Any brigade attack going forward from here would pass over and around Big Round Top, then arrive south and southeast of Little Round Top. From there the right regiments of the attacking brigade could flank or bypass the Union defenses.

You are in the center of where Law's Brigade was after it deployed for attack. The Fifteenth Alabama was where you are. To your right were the Forty-fourth and then Forty-eighth Alabama. To your left were the Forty-seventh and then the Fourth Alabama. Four hundred yards behind you Brigadier General Henry L. Benning deployed his four Georgia regiments to support Law's attack.

As Law's regiments attacked across the open ground in front of you, they began to receive fire from Captain James E. Smith's Fourth New York Battery, located on the ground just above Devil's Den. In response to this fire, Law ordered his two right regiments, the Forty-fourth and Forty-eight, out of line and had them cross behind the three regiments to their left in order to attack Smith's battery.

When Benning's Brigade, following behind Law's, came forward, it moved through the trees that are behind you and to your right rear. As Benning came out of the trees, he saw the Forty-fourth and Forty-eighth

Alabama as they departed from the line of attack and moved toward Devil's Den. Not seeing Law's other three regiments as they went on toward the Round Tops, Benning shifted his direction of movement to the left and followed the Forty-fourth and Forty-eighth Alabama. This shift carried Benning into the fight for Devil's Den. Had he continued moving straight ahead, behind Law's other three regiments, Benning would have been in position to support the flanking attack against the defenses on Little Round Top or isolate the position by moving east a short distance.

Report of Brig. Gen. Henry L. Benning, CSA, Commanding Benning's Brigade, Hood's Division, Longstreet's Corps, Army of Northern Virginia

About 2 or 3 P.M. on July 2, ultimo, I was informed by Major-General Hood that his division, as the right of Lieutenant-General Longstreet's corps, was about to attack the left of the enemy's line, and that in the attack my brigade would follow Law's brigade at the distance of about 400 yards. In order to get to the place they assigned me, in the rear of General Law, it was necessary to move the brigade 500 or 600 yards farther to the right. Having done this, I advanced in line of battle. A wood intervened between us and the enemy, which, though it did not prevent their shells from reaching us and producing some casualties, yet completely hid them from our view. On emerging from the woods, their position became visible. Before us, at the distance of [1,100] yards, was [Devil's Den] presenting to us a steep face, much roughened by rocks. To the right, 400 or 500 yards [was Little Round Top], with a side that looked almost perpendicular. Its summit overlooked [Devil's Den] just sufficiently to command it well. On the summit of [Devil's Den] were [four] pieces of artillery. To the right and left of the battery, as well as immediately in its rear, were lines of infantry, as we afterward ascertained. This formed the enemy's first line of battle.

On the top of [Little Round Top] were five other guns. These commanded our approaches for nearly the whole way. To the right and left of these guns extended the enemy's second line of infantry. Where that line crossed the gorge running between [Devil's Den and Little Round Top], a point 500 or 600 yards in the rear, were two other guns. This we ascertained when the right of the brigade reached the gorge, by the terrible fire from them which swept down the gorge.

Thus, what we had to encounter were [eleven] guns, and two, if not more, lines of infantry posted on the heights. The intervening spur over which we had to march to reach the first line was nearly all open. Our own first line also became visible advancing about 400 yards in our front. The part of it in our front I took to be Law's brigade, and so I followed it. In truth, it was Robertson's, Law's being farther to the right. This I did not discover until late in the fight, a wood on the right concealing from me most of Law's brigade. My line continued to follow the first line, halting once or twice to preserve its interval. At length I saw that the first line would not be able alone to carry the [enemy position], so I advanced without halting again. [*OR*, vol. 27, pt. 2, 414–15]

Lee's had planned for a two-division, eight-brigade envelopment of the Union left. Late in the afternoon his plan was reduced to just two brigades. If there was to be an envelopment of the Union's left, Law's and Benning's Brigades were the only ones potentially in position to do so. However, these combined decisions negated even that possibility as the combat power that was initially in the right of Hood's attack was shifted toward his division's center. There they frontally attacked Union forces in a defensive position instead of striking an overwhelming blow on the flank of the defenses.

Return to your car for the drive to Stop 12.

The distance to Stop 12 is 4.1 miles. Drive on South Confederate Avenue for 1.2 miles to a road intersection. You drove past Big Round Top and are now at the south base of Little Round Top. Continue driving for 0.1 mile to the crest of Little Round Top. If you wish, you can stop here and walk to the western edge of the hill where you can look back toward Stops 8, 9, 10, and 11. From the top of Little Round Top, continue driving north for 0.2 mile. Just as you come down off the northern slope, you will arrive at a road intersection. Turn right and drive east for 0.1 mile to another road intersection. This is the Taneytown Road. Turn left on the Taneytown Road, and drive north for 0.7 mile to an intersection with a road from the right. Look carefully as this road is easy to miss. This is Granite School House Lane. Turn right on to Granite School House Lane, and drive 0.6 mile to the intersection with Blacksmith Shop Road. Turn left and drive 0.1 mile to the intersection with the Baltimore Pike. Turn left on to the Baltimore Pike, and drive 0.2 mile to the park road on your right. There are signs indicating that this road goes to Spangler's Spring and Culp's Hill. Turn right on this road, and drive for 0.5 mile to Spangler's Spring. At the spring there is a road that comes from the right. This is East Confederate Avenue. Drive past this road, and start up Culp's Hill. You will come to a Y in the road. Take the right fork (Slocum Avenue), and continue driving up the hill. Drive for 0.3 mile to another Y in the road. Take the right fork, and drive for 200 yards. Park so that all four wheels of your car are on the road. Leave your car and walk east (your right as you drove) to the line of monuments. Find the monument for the 78th and 102d New York Regiments. Stand beside the monument.

Stop 12—Greene Remains on Culp's Hill, July 2, 1863

You are in the center of the position held by Brigadier General George S. Greene's Third Brigade, Second Division, Twelfth Corps, after he extended his brigade to his right to cover as much ground as possible. To your left the ground rises up to the apex of the hill (Upper Culp's Hill). To your right the ground falls away to a terrain saddle, then rises again to Lower Culp's Hill. The ground in front of you descends steeply and is covered with woods, as it was in 1863.

Brigadier General John Geary's Second Division initially occupied a position with Greene's brigade on the left and Brigadier General Thomas L. Kane's Second Brigade on the right. Geary's troops faced to the east and northeast. Greene's position went from the top of Upper Culp's Hill, to your left, past where you are, and continued to your right to the lower part of the hill. Kane's brigade occupied the position to Greene's right, where the ground ascends to Lower Culp's Hill, with a forward and a supporting line. Colonel Charles Candy's First Brigade was in a reserve position to the rear of your location.

Brigadier General Alpheus S. Williams's First Division, Twelfth Corps (commanded by Brigadier General Thomas H. Ruger while Williams temporarily commanded the corps), was on Geary's right. Ruger's troops faced northeast, east, and south. Ruger's left brigade was led by Colonel Archibald L. McDougall. With a forward and a supporting line it joined with Kane's right on Lower Culp's Hill. Colonel Silas Colgrove's brigade was to McDougall's right. Brigadier General Henry H. Lockwood's brigade, on Colgrove's right, occupied a position at a right angle to the corps. Lockwood's regiments faced south, with the right of his position near the Baltimore Pike so as to protect the corps and the army's right flank. Part of Colgrove's brigade and Lockwood's entire brigade were south of Spangler's Spring, which is in the lower ground on the other (south) side of Lower Culp's Hill.

The survivors from the July 1 combat of Brigadier General James Wadsworth's First Division, First Corps, were on the Twelfth Corps' and Greene's left flank. Wadsworth's position went from the top of Upper Culp's Hill to the west for 300 yards. His troops faced north and covered the northern approaches to the hill.

Report of Brig. Gen. George S. Greene, USA, Commanding Third Brigade, Second Division, Twelfth Corps, Army of the Potomac

On the 2d, we took position at about 6 A.M. on the right of the First Corps, on the crest of the steep and rocky hill, being thrown back nearly at right angles with the line of the First Corps, Rock Creek running past our front at the distance of 200 to 400 yards. Our position and the front were covered with a heavy growth of timber, free from undergrowth, with large ledges of rock projecting above the surface. These rocks and trees offered good cover for marksmen. The surface was very steep on our left, diminishing to a gentle slope on our right. The Second Brigade was on our right, thrown forward at a right angle to conform to the crest of the hill. On the right of this brigade was the First (Williams') Division, his right resting on an impassable mill-pond on Rock Creek. As soon as we were in position, we began to intrench ourselves and throw up breastworks of the covering height, of logs, cord-wood, stones, and earth. The same was done by the troops on my right.

By 12 o'clock we had a good cover for the men. The value of this defense was shown in our subsequent operations by our small loss compared with that of the enemy during the continuous attacks by a vastly superior force. Our skirmishers were thrown out immediately on taking position, and moved toward the creek in our front, when they came to the enemy's pickets. [*OR*, vol. 27, pt. 1, 855–56]

When Longstreet's divisions and Anderson's Division struck Meade's left and left center, the defenses began to collapse. Looking for reinforcements to prevent a Confederate breakthrough, Meade ordered the two Twelfth Corps divisions on Culp's Hill to leave their positions and redeploy to the army's left and left center. Ruger's (Williams's) division was the first to leave, departing between 6:00 and 6:30 P.M. Thirty minutes later Geary was ordered to follow Ruger. As Greene's brigade was preparing to depart, the skirmish line reported a large Confederate force approaching. Greene ordered his regiments to remain in position as the rest of Geary's division marched away. About the same time, Colonel Hiram C. Rodgers of the Twelfth Corps staff arrived with orders for Greene's brigade to remain in position.

Greene realized that he could not occupy both Upper and Lower Culp's Hill. However, Upper Culp's Hill, being the higher of the two hills and also having Wadsworth's division there, was tactically the most important. Control of the higher hill would dominate any Confederate positions lower down and protect the army's right flank and the Baltimore Pike. After the other five brigades of the corps departed, Greene extended his defensive line to his right to occupy some of the abandoned position. After this was accomplished, Greene's regiments were in position with the 60th New York on the brigade left, near the apex of Upper Culp's Hill. To their right was the 102d New York. In the center (about where you are) was the 78th New York. The 149th New York was to the 78th's right, in the lower ground. The 137th New York was the right flank regiment. Initially its position went from the low ground to Lower Culp's Hill. However, as the Confederate attack developed, this regiment was redeployed across the low ground to your right, faced south, and protected the brigade's right flank.

Report of Brig. Gen. George S. Greene, USA—Continued

We remained in this position, with occasional firing of the pickets, until 6.30 P.M., when the First (Williams') Division and the First and Second Brigades of the Second Division were ordered from my right, leaving the intrenchments of Kane's brigade and Williams' division unoccupied on the withdrawal of the troops.

I received orders to occupy the whole of the intrenchments previously occupied by the Twelfth Army Corps with my brigade. This movement was commenced, and the One hundred and thirty-seventh Regiment, on my right, was moved into the position occupied by Kane's (Second) brigade. Before any further movements could be made, we were attacked on the whole of our front by a large force a few minutes before 7 P.M. The enemy made four distinct charges between 7 and 9.30 P.M., which were effectually resisted.

About 8 P.M. the enemy appeared on our right flank, in the intrenchments (which were thrown back perpendicularly to Kane's line, occupied by Colonel Ireland with the One hundred and thirty-seventh Regiment New York Volunteers) from which Williams' division had been withdrawn, and attacked the right flank of the One hundred and thirty-seventh Regiment New York Volunteers. Colonel Ireland withdrew his right, throwing back his line perpendicular to the intrenchments in which he had been in position, and presenting his front to the enemy in their new position. [*OR*, vol. 27, pt. 1, 856]

Lee's July 2 plan was for Longstreet's two divisions supported by Anderson's Division to make the main attack on Meade's left flank. Simultaneously, Lieutenant General Richard S. Ewell was to conduct a demonstration and if feasible turn that into an actual attack. Ewell's attack was to prevent Meade from using the units on Culp's Hill and East Cemetery to reinforce his left flank and also to capture the key terrain of Culp's Hill and/or Cemetery Hill.

Ewell began his demonstration with an artillery battalion firing on East Cemetery Hill. This was followed by an attack with two brigades of Major General Jubal Early's division against East Cemetery Hill. This attack was unsuccessful. At the same time, Major General Edward Johnson sent three of his four brigades up the east side of Culp's Hill. Two of his brigades, Jones's and Nicholls's (Williams's), frontally attacked Greene's position. The third brigade, Steuart's, hit the south (right) section of the defensive position and maneuvered to outflank Greene. They were halted when the 137th New York swung its line back so as to face south. However, Steuart did control Lower Culp's Hill.

Report of Maj. Gen. Edward Johnson, CSA, Commanding Johnson's Division, Ewell's Corps, Army of Northern Virginia

In obedience to an order from the lieutenant-general commanding, I then advanced my infantry to the assault of the enemy's strong position—a rugged and rocky mountain, heavily timbered and difficult of ascent; a natural fortification, rendered more formidable by deep intrenchments and thick abates—Jones' brigade in advance, followed by Nicholls' and Steuart's. General Walker was directed to follow, but reporting to me that the enemy were advancing upon

> him from their right, he was ordered to repulse them and follow on as soon as possible.
>
> By the time my other brigades had crossed Rock Creek and reached the base of the mountain, it was dark. His skirmishers were driven in, and the attack made with great vigor and spirit. It was as successful as could have been expected, considering the enemy's force and position. Steuart's brigade, on the left, carried a line of breastworks which ran perpendicular to the enemy's main line, captured a number of prisoners and a stand of colors, and the whole line advanced to within short range, and kept up a heavy fire until late in the night. [*OR*, vol. 27, pt. 2, 504]

Johnson's attack was too late to prevent Meade from using brigades on Culp's Hill as reinforcement for the threatened left and left center of his position. Although his attack was halted by darkness, Johnson did control Lower Culp's Hill. His division was positioned to continue the attack the next morning, but Johnson's freedom of action as to when and where he could attack was lost by a decision made on the night of July 2–3.

Return to your car for the drive to Stop 13.

Continue driving on Slocum Avenue for 0.1 mile to a T intersection. If you wish to go to the apex of Culp's Hill, turn right and follow the road for 100 yards. Otherwise turn left at the T intersection and drive for 0.25 mile to the intersection with a road to the left. Turn left on to this road, and drive west 150 yards to the Baltimore Pike. Turn left onto the Baltimore Pike, and drive slightly over 0.5 mile to the entrance to the Visitor Center. Turn right, and park in one of the Visitor Center parking lots. From the Visitor Center, walk north a short distance to an east-west park road. This is Hunt Avenue. At Hunt Avenue turn right and walk east parallel to, but off, the road to the stone markers for Battery F, 4th U.S. Artillery, and Battery K, 5th U.S. Artillery. Be extremely careful of traffic. Stand off the road in a safe place, and look east toward the Baltimore Pike.

Stop 13—Slocum and Williams Steal the Initiative, July 3, 1863

The high ground to your left front, covered with trees, is Culp's Hill. McAllister's Hill is 400 yards to your right front. The high ground to your right is Powers Hill. The Baltimore Pike is the road in front of you. It was the main supply and communication route for the Army of the Potomac. Major General Henry W. Slocum's headquarters was located this side of the pike and 700 yards (0.4 mile) to your right. Slocum was acting temporarily in the capacity as the right-wing commander. As such he had responsibility for all troops on or in close proximity to Culp's Hill. This included his own Twelfth Corps, temporarily commanded by Brigadier Alpheus Williams, and one division from the First Corps.

Late in the afternoon of July 2, Meade had moved most of the Twelfth Corps toward his left center to assist in the defense. The First Corps division and Brigadier General George S. Greene's brigade had been left in defensive positions on the highest part of the hill. Soon thereafter Ewell had Major General Edward Johnson's division attack to capture Culp's Hill. This attack, if successful, would have placed Confederate forces in a position to cut the Baltimore Pike and given them access to the rear areas of Meade's army. Johnson's troops were able to capture the lower part of the hill, but the top was still in Union hands. Returning after dark to reoccupy their positions, the Union regiments found them controlled by Johnson's troops. Slocum ordered William to deploy into attack position during the night and then attack to regain the lost ground at first light. The attack was to be preceded by a fifteen-minute artillery preparation.

Under Williams's command were two infantry divisions and five artillery batteries, his four and one from the artillery reserve, with a total of twenty-six guns. Two of the guns were located on McAllister's Hill, fourteen were on Powers Hill, and ten were positioned where you are. The position of Brigadier General John W. Geary's division went from the top of Culp's Hill south for a short distance and then southwest almost to the Baltimore Pike. Williams's division, commanded by Brigadier General Thomas H. Ruger, was positioned with one brigade to your immediate left on this side of the pike. The other two brigades were on the other side of the pike and facing in a northerly direction. From there they could maneuver against the south part of Culp's Hill.

During the night Johnson was reinforced with two brigades from Rodes's Division and one brigade from Early's Division. He had been ordered to resume his attack at first light as part of Lee's initial plan for July 3.

Report of Maj. Gen. Edward Johnson, CSA, Commanding Johnson's Division, Ewell's Corps, Army of Northern Virginia

Early next morning, the Stonewall Brigade was ordered to the support of the others, and the assault was renewed with great determination. Shortly after, the enemy moved forward to recapture the line of breastworks which had been taken the night previous, but was repulsed with great slaughter. Daniel's and Rodes' brigades (Colonel [E. A.] O'Neal commanding), of Rodes' division, having reported to me, two other assaults were made; both failed. The enemy were too securely intrenched and in too great numbers to be dislodged by the force at my command.

In the meantime, a demonstration in force was made upon my left and rear. The Second Virginia Regiment, Stonewall Brigade, and Smith's brigade, of Early's division, were disposed to meet and check it, which was accomplished to my entire satisfaction. No further assault was made; all had been done that it was possible to do.

I held my original position until 10 o'clock of the night of the 3d, when, in accordance with orders, I withdrew to the hill north and west of Gettysburg, where we remained until the following day, in the hope that the enemy would give us battle on ground of our own selection.

My loss in this terrible battle was heavy, including some of the most valuable officers of the command.

The casualties in my division during the operations around Gettysburg were: Killed, 219; Wounded, 1,229; Missing, 375; Total, 1,823. [*OR*, vol. 27, pt. 2, 504–6]

Sunrise was at 4:45 A.M., but it was light enough to begin operations one-half hour prior. The Twelfth Corps artillery opened fire at 4:30 A.M. The artillery fire lasted for fifteen minutes and then ceased to allow the infantry to attack. However, before the Twelfth Corps infantry had moved very far, Johnson commenced his attack. Although Johnson was scheduled to attack that morning, the Union artillery fire forced him to attack immediately at first light. This deprived Johnson of the ability to decide exactly when to attack. His reinforced division conducted three attacks against the defenders on Culp's Hill. None of them was successful, and at 10:30 A.M. Johnson ceased attacking and ordered his units into defensive position at the base of Culp's Hill.

Report of Maj. Gen. Henry W. Slocum, USA, Commanding Twelfth Corps, Army of the Potomac

Orders were at once issued for an attack at daybreak, for the purpose of regaining that portion of the line which had been lost. The artillery of the Twelfth Corps was placed in position during the night by Lieutenant-Colonel Best, and opened the battle at 4 A.M. on the following morning, and during the entire engagement all these batteries rendered most valuable aid to our cause.

The enemy had been re-enforced during the night, and were fully prepared to resist our attack. The force opposed to us, it is said, belonged to the corps under General Ewell. We were re-enforced during the engagement by Shaler's brigade, of the Sixth Corps, and by two regiments from General Wadsworth's division, of the First Corps, and also by Neill's brigade, of the Sixth Corps, which was moved across Rock Creek, and placed in position to protect our extreme right. All these troops did excellent service.

The engagement continued until 10.30 A.M., and resulted in our regaining possession of our entire line of intrenchments and driving the enemy back of the position originally held by him; in the capture of over 500 prisoners in addition to the large number of wounded left on the field, besides several thousand stand of arms and three stand of colors. Our own loss in killed and wounded was comparatively light, as most of our troops were protected by breastworks. [*OR*, vol. 27, pt. 1, 761]

The Union right flank had been stabilized and the threat to the Baltimore Pike removed. Johnson's Division was fought out and unable to provide support to the assault against the center of Meade's defenses.

Slocum's order to "drive them out at first light" and Williams's immediate preparations to position his artillery and infantry for an attack at first light took the initiative away from Ewell and Johnson. Johnson was also prepared to attack, with the decision as to when being his. Williams's pre-attack artillery fire took the initiative from him and forced Johnson to order his brigades forward. When Ewell received word that Lee had postponed the early morning attack, it was too late to stop Johnson. More important, once his units became decisively engaged, Williams's aggressiveness precluded the possibility of Johnson breaking contact and withdrawing in order to be available to support the afternoon Confederate attack. As Lee began to formulate his final plan for July 3, the left of his army was decisively engaged and repulsed with such loss as to render them unusable for the rest of the day. This severely limited the force Lee had available for any offensive action he might chose.

This completes your tour. Return to the Visitor Center. If you would like to do a comprehensive tour of the battle, I recommend Jay Luvaas and Harold Nelson's *The U.S. Army War College Guide to the Battle of Gettysburg* and Mark Grimsley and Brook D. Simpson's *Gettysburg: A Battlefield Guide.* For a comprehensive tour and study of the artillery at Gettysburg, try my book *Summer Thunder: A Battlefield Guide to the Artillery at Gettysburg.*

APPENDIX II

UNION ORDER OF BATTLE

ARMY OF THE POTOMAC
   Maj. Gen. George G. Meade

FIRST ARMY CORPS
   Maj. Gen. John F. Reynolds
   Maj. Gen. Abner Doubleday
   Maj. Gen. John Newton

FIRST DIVISION
   Brig. Gen. James S. Wadsworth

FIRST BRIGADE
   Brig. Gen. Solomon Meredith
   Col. William W. Robinson
   19th Indiana
   24th Michigan
   2d Wisconsin
   6th Wisconsin
   7th Wisconsin

SECOND BRIGADE
   Brig. Gen. Lysander Cutler
   7th Indiana
   76th New York

84th New York
95th New York
147th New York
56th Pennsylvania

SECOND DIVISION
Brig. Gen. John C. Robinson

FIRST BRIGADE
Brig. Gen. Gabriel R. Paul
Col. Samuel H. Leonard
Col. Adrian Root
Col Richard Coulter
16th Maine
13th Massachusetts
94th New York
104th New York
107th Pennsylvania

SECOND BRIGADE
Brig. Gen. Henry Baxter
12th Massachusetts
83d New York
97th New York
11th Pennsylvania
88th Pennsylvania
90th Pennsylvania

THIRD DIVISION
Maj. Gen. Abner Doubleday
Brig. Gen. Thomas A. Rowley
Maj. Gen. Abner Doubleday

FIRST BRIGADE
Col. Chapman Biddle
Brig. Gen. Thomas A. Rowley
Col. Chapman Biddle
80th New York
121st Pennsylvania
142d Pennsylvania
151st Pennsylvania

SECOND BRIGADE
Col. Roy Stone
Col. Langhorne Wister
Col. Edmund L. Dana
143d Pennsylvania
149th Pennsylvania
150th Pennsylvania

THIRD BRIGADE
Brig. Gen. George J. Stannard
Col. Francis V. Randall
12th Vermont
13th Vermont
14th Vermont
15th Vermont
16th Vermont

ARTILLERY BRIGADE
Col. Charles S. Wainwright
2d Maine Battery
5th Maine Battery
Battery L, 1st New York
Battery B, 1st Pennsylvania
Battery B, 4th United States

SECOND ARMY CORPS
Maj. Gen. Winfield S. Hancock
Brig. Gen. John Gibbon

FIRST DIVISION
Brig. Gen. John C. Caldwell

FIRST BRIGADE
Col. Edward E. Cross
Col. H. Boyd McKeen
5th New Hampshire
61st New York
81st Pennsylvania
148th Pennsylvania

SECOND BRIGADE
Col. Patrick Kelly

28th Massachusetts
63d New York (2 companies)
69th New York (2 companies)
88th New York (2 companies)
116th Pennsylvania (4 companies)

THIRD BRIGADE
Brig. Gen. Samuel K. Zook
Lieut. Col. John Fraser
52d New York
57th New York
66th New York
140th Pennsylvania

FOURTH BRIGADE
Col. John R. Brooke
27th Connecticut (2 companies)
2d Delaware
64th New York
53d Pennsylvania
145th Pennsylvania (7 companies)

SECOND DIVISION
Brig. Gen. John Gibbon
Brig. Gen. William Harrow

FIRST BRIGADE
Brig. Gen. William Harrow
Col. Francis E. Heath
19th Maine
15th Massachusetts
1st Minnesota
82d New York

SECOND BRIGADE
Brig. Gen. Alexander S. Webb
69th Pennsylvania
71st Pennsylvania
72d Pennsylvania
106th Pennsylvania

THIRD BRIGADE
Col. Norman J. Hall

19th Massachusetts
20th Massachusetts
7th Michigan
42d New York
59th New York (4 companies)

THIRD DIVISION
Brig. Gen. Alexander Hays

FIRST BRIGADE
Col. Samuel S. Carroll
14th Indiana
4th Ohio
8th Ohio
7th West Virginia

SECOND BRIGADE
Col. Thomas A. Smyth
Lieut. Col. Francis E. Pierce
14th Connecticut
1st Delaware
12th New Jersey
10th New York
108th New York

THIRD BRIGADE
Col. George L. Willard
Col. Eliakim Sherrill
Lieut. Col. James M. Bull
39th New York (4 companies)
111th New York
125th New York
126th New York

ARTILLERY BRIGADE
Capt. John G. Hazard
Battery B, 1st New York
Battery A, 1st Rhode Island
Battery B, 1st Rhode Island
Battery I, 1st United States
Battery A, 4th United States

THIRD ARMY CORPS
Maj. Gen. Daniel E. Sickles
Maj. Gen. David B. Burney

FIRST DIVISION
Maj. Gen. David B. Birney
Brig. Gen. J. H. Hobart Ward

FIRST BRIGADE
Brig. Gen. Charles K. Graham
Col. Andrew H. Tippin
57th Pennsylvania (8 companies)
63d Pennsylvania
68th Pennsylvania
105th Pennsylvania
114th Pennsylvania
141st Pennsylvania

SECOND BRIGADE
Brig. Gen. J. H. Hobart Ward
Col. Hiram Berdan
20th Indiana
3d Maine
4th Maine
86th New York
124th New York
99th Pennsylvania
1st U.S. Sharpshooters
2d U.S. Sharpshooters (8 companies)

THIRD BRIGADE
Col. P. Regis De Trobriand
17th Maine
3d Michigan
5th Michigan
40th New York
110th Pennsylvania (6 companies)

SECOND DIVISION
Brig. Gen. Andrew A. Humphreys

FIRST BRIGADE
Brig. Gen. Joseph B. Carr
1st Massachusetts
11th Massachusetts
16th Massachusetts
12th New Hampshire
11th New Jersey
26th Pennsylvania
84th Pennsylvania

SECOND BRIGADE
Col. William R. Brewster
70th New York
71st New York
72d New York
73d New York
74th New York
120th New York

THIRD BRIGADE
Col. George C. Burling
2d New Hampshire
5th New Jersey
6th New Jersey
7th New Jersey
8th New Jersey
115th Pennsylvania

ARTILLERY BRIGADE
Capt. George E. Randolph
Capt. A. Judson Clark
2d New Jersey Battery
Battery D, 1st New York
4th New York Battery
Battery E, 1st Rhode Island
Battery K, 4th United States

FIFTH ARMY CORPS
Maj. Gen. George Sykes

FIRST DIVISION
    Brig. Gen. James Barnes

FIRST BRIGADE
    Col. William S. Tilton
    18th Massachusetts
    22d Massachusetts
    1st Michigan
    118th Pennsylvania

SECOND BRIGADE
    Col. Jacob B. Sweitzer
    9th Massachusetts
    32d Massachusetts
    4th Michigan
    62d Pennsylvania

THIRD BRIGADE
    Col. Strong Vincent
    Col. James C. Rice
    20th Maine
    16th Michigan
    44th New York
    83d Pennsylvania

SECOND DIVISION
    Brig. Gen Romeyn B. Ayers

FIRST BRIGADE
    Col. Hannibal Day
    3d United States (6 companies)
    4th United States (4 companies)
    6th United States (5 companies)
    12th United States (8 companies)
    14th United States (8 companies)

SECOND BRIGADE
    Col. Sidney Burbank
    2d United States (6 companies)
    7th United States (4 companies)
    10th United States (3 companies)
    11th United States (6 companies)
    17th United States (7 companies)

THIRD BRIGADE
Brig. Gen. Stephen H. Weed
Col. Kenner Garrard
140th New York
146th New York
91st Pennsylvania
155th Pennsylvania

THIRD DIVISION
Brig. Gen. Samuel W. Crawford

FIRST BRIGADE
Col. William McCandless
1st Pennsylvania Reserves (9 companies)
2d Pennsylvania Reserves
6th Pennsylvania Reserves
13th Pennsylvania Reserves

THIRD BRIGADE
Col. Joseph W. Fisher
5th Pennsylvania Reserves
9th Pennsylvania Reserves
10th Pennsylvania Reserves
11th Pennsylvania Reserves
12th Pennsylvania Reserves (9 companies)

ARTILLERY BRIGADE
Capt. Augustus P. Martin
3d Massachusetts Battery
Battery C, 1st New York
Battery L, 1st Ohio
Battery D, 5th United States
Battery I, 5th United States

SIXTH ARMY CORPS
Maj. Gen. John Sedgwick

FIRST DIVISION
Brig. Gen. Horatio G. Wright

FIRST BRIGADE
Brig. Gen. Alfred T. A. Torbert

1st New Jersey
2d New Jersey
3d New Jersey
15th New Jersey

SECOND BRIGADE

Brig. Gen. Joseph J. Bartlett
5th Maine
121st New York
95th Pennsylvania
96th Pennsylvania

THIRD BRIGADE

Brig. Gen. David A. Russell
6th Maine
49th Pennsylvania (4 companies)
119th Pennsylvania
5th Wisconsin

SECOND DIVISION

Brig. Gen. Albion P. Howe

SECOND BRIGADE

Col. Lewis A. Grant
2d Vermont
3d Vermont
4th Vermont
5th Vermont
6th Vermont

THIRD BRIGADE

Brig. Gen. Thomas H. Neill
7th Maine (6 companies)
33d New York
43d New York
49th New York
77th New York
61st Pennsylvania

THIRD DIVISION

Maj. Gen. John Newton
Brig. Gen Frank Wheaton

FIRST BRIGADE
Brig. Gen. Alexander Shaler
65th New York
67th New York
122d New York
23d Pennsylvania
82d Pennsylvania

SECOND BRIGADE
Col. Henry L. Eustis
7th Massachusetts
10th Massachusetts
37th Massachusetts
2d Rhode Island

THIRD BRIGADE
Brig. Gen. Frank Wheaton
Col. David J. Nevin
62d New York
93d Pennsylvania
98th Pennsylvania
102d Pennsylvania
139th Pennsylvania

ARTILLERY BRIGADE
Col. Charles H. Tompkins
1st Massachusetts Battery
1st New York Battery
3d New York Battery
Battery C, 1st Rhode Island
Battery G, 1st Rhode Island
Battery D, 2d United States
Battery G, 2d United States
Battery F, 5th United States

ELEVENTH ARMY CORPS
Maj. Gen. Oliver O. Howard

FIRST DIVISION
Brig. Gen. Francis C. Barlow
Brig. Gen. Adelbert Ames

FIRST BRIGADE
Col. Leopold Von Gilsa
41st New York (9 companies)
54th New York
68th New York
153d Pennsylvania

SECOND BRIGADE
Brig. Gen. Adelbert Ames
Col. Andrew L. Harris
17th Connecticut
25th Ohio
75th Ohio
107th Ohio

SECOND DIVISION
Brig. Gen. Adolph Von Steinwehr

FIRST BRIGADE
Col. Charles R. Coster
134th New York
154th New York
27th Pennsylvania
73d Pennsylvania

SECOND BRIGADE
Col. Orlando Smith
33d Massachusetts
136th New York
55th Ohio
73d Ohio

THIRD DIVISION
Maj. Gen. Carl Schurz

FIRST BRIGADE
Brig. Gen. Alexander Schimmelfennig
Col. George Von Amsberg
82d Illinois
45th New York
157th New York
61st Ohio
74th Pennsylvania

SECOND BRIGADE
>   Col. Wladimir Krzyzanowski
>   58th New York
>   119th New York
>   82d Ohio
>   75th Pennsylvania
>   26th Wisconsin

ARTILLERY BRIGADE
>   Maj. Thomas W. Osborn
>   Battery I, 1st New York
>   13th New York Battery
>   Battery I, 1st Ohio
>   Battery K, 1st Ohio
>   Battery G, 4th United States

TWELFTH ARMY CORPS
>   Maj. Gen. Henry W. Slocum
>   Brig. Gen. Alpheus S. Williams

FIRST DIVISION
>   Brig. Gen. Alpheus S. Williams
>   Brig. Gen. Thomas H. Ruger

FIRST BRIGADE
>   Col. Archibald L. McDougall
>   5th Connecticut
>   20th Connecticut
>   3d Maryland
>   123d New York
>   145th New York
>   46th Pennsylvania

SECOND BRIGADE
>   Brig. Gen. Henry H. Lockwood
>   1st Maryland, Potomac Home
>   1st Maryland, Eastern Shore
>   150th New York

THIRD BRIGADE
>   Brig. Gen. Thomas H. Ruger
>   Col. Silas Colgrove
>   27th Indiana
>   2d Massachusetts

13th New Jersey
107th New York
3d Wisconsin

SECOND DIVISION
Brig. Gen John W. Geary

FIRST BRIGADE
Col. Charles Candy
5th Ohio
7th Ohio
29th Ohio
66th Ohio
28th Pennsylvania
147th Pennsylvania (8 companies)

SECOND BRIGADE
Col. George A. Cobham
Brig. Gen. Thomas Kane
Col. George A. Cobham
29th Pennsylvania
109th Pennsylvania
111th Pennsylvania

THIRD BRIGADE
Brig. Gen. George S. Greene
60th New York
78th New York
102d New York
137th New York
149th New York

ARTILLERY BRIGADE
Lieut. Edward D. Muhlenberg
Battery M, 1st New York
Battery E, Pennsylvania
Battery F, 4th United States
Battery K, 5th United States

CAVALRY CORPS
Maj. Gen. Alfred Pleasonton

FIRST DIVISION
   Brig. Gen. John Buford

FIRST BRIGADE
   Col. William Gamble
   8th Illinois
   12th Illinois (4 companies)
   3d Indiana (6 companies)
   8th New York
SECOND BRIGADE
   Col. Thomas C. Devin
   6th New York
   9th New York
   17th Pennsylvania
   3d West Virginia (2 companies)
RESERVE BRIGADE
   Brig. Gen. Wesley Merritt
   6th Pennsylvania
   1st United States
   2d United States
   5th United States
   6th United States

SECOND DIVISION
   Brig. Gen. David McM. Gregg

FIRST BRIGADE
   Col. John B. McIntosh
   1st Maryland (11 companies)
   Company A, Purnell (Maryland) Legion
   1st Massachusetts
   1st New Jersey
   1st Pennsylvania
   3d Pennsylvania
   Section, Battery H, 3d Pennsylvania Heavy Artillery
SECOND BRIGADE
   Col. Pennock Huey
   2d New York
   4th New York

6th Ohio (10 companies)
8th Pennsylvania

THIRD BRIGADE
Col. J. Irving Gregg
1st Maine (10 companies)
10th New York
4th Pennsylvania
16th Pennsylvania

THIRD DIVISION
Brig. Gen. Judson Kilpatrick

FIRST BRIGADE
Brig. Gen. Elon J. Farnsworth
Col. Nathaniel P. Richmond
5th New York
18th Pennsylvania
1st Vermont
1st West Virginia (10 companies)

SECOND BRIGADE
Brig. Gen. George A. Custer
1st Michigan
5th Michigan
6th Michigan
7th Michigan (10 companies)

HORSE ARTILLERY

FIRST BRIGADE
Capt. James M. Robertson
9th Michigan Battery
6th New York Battery
Batteries B & L, 2d United States
Battery M, 2d United States
Battery E, 4th United States

SECOND BRIGADE
Capt. John C. Tidball
Batteries E & G, 1st United States
Battery K, 1st United States

Battery A, 2d United States
Battery C, 3d United States

ARTILLERY RESERVE
Brig. Gen. Robert O. Tyler

FIRST REGULAR BRIGADE
Capt. Dunbar R. Ransom
Battery H, 1st United States
Batteries F & K, 3d United States
Battery C, 4th United States
Battery C , 5th United States

FIRST VOLUNTEER BRIGADE
Lieut. Col. Freeman McGilvery
5th Massachusetts Battery
9th Massachusetts Battery
15th New York Battery
Batteries C & F, Pennsylvania

SECOND VOLUNTEER BRIGADE
Capt. Elijah D. Taft
Battery B, 1st Connecticut Heavy
Battery M, 1st Connecticut Heavy
2d Connecticut Battery
5th New York Battery

THIRD VOLUNTEER BRIGADE
Capt. James F. Huntington
1st New Hampshire Battery
Battery H, 1st Ohio
Batteries F & G, 1st Pennsylvania
Battery C, West Virginia

FOURTH VOLUNTEER BRIGADE
Capt. Robert H. Fitzhugh
6th Maine Battery
Battery A, Maryland
1st New Jersey Battery
Battery G, 1st New York
Battery K, 1st New York

[*OR*, vol. 27, pt. 1, pp. 155–68]

APPENDIX III

CONFEDERATE ORDER OF BATTLE

ARMY OF NORTHERN VIRGINIA
Gen. Robert E. Lee

LONGSTREET'S CORPS
Lieut. Gen. James Longstreet

McLAWS'S DIVISION
Maj. Gen. Lafayette McLaws

KERSHAW'S BRIGADE
Brig. Gen. Joseph B. Kershaw
2d South Carolina
3d South Carolina
7th South Carolina
8th South Carolina
15th South Carolina
3d South Carolina Battalion

BARKSDALE'S BRIGADE
Brig. Gen. William Barksdale
Col. Benjamin G. Humphreys
13th Mississippi

17th Mississippi
18th Mississippi
21st Mississippi

SEMMES'S BRIGADE
Brig. Gen. Paul J. Semmes
Col. Goode Bryant
10th Georgia
50th Georgia
51st Georgia
53d Georgia

WOFFORD'S BRIGADE
Brig. Gen. William T. Wofford
16th Georgia
18th Georgia
24th Georgia
Cobb's (Georgia) Legion
Phillips (Georgia) Legion

ARTILLERY
Col. Henry C. Cabell
Battery A, 1st North Carolina
Pulaski (Georgia) Artillery
1st Richmond Howitzers
Troup (Georgia) Artillery

PICKETT'S DIVISION
Maj. Gen. George E. Pickett

GARNETT'S BRIGADE
Brig. Gen. Richard B. Garnett
Maj. Charles S. Peyton
8th Virginia
18th Virginia
19th Virginia
28th Virginia
56th Virginia

KEMPER'S BRIGADE
Brig. Gen. James L. Kemper
Col. Joseph Mayo, Jr.
1st Virginia

3d Virginia
7th Virginia
11th Virginia
24th Virginia

ARMISTEAD'S BRIGADE

Brig. Gen. Louis A. Armistead
Col. William R. Aylett
9th Virginia
14th Virginia
38th Virginia
53d Virginia
57th Virginia

ARTILLERY

Maj. James Dearing
Fauquier (Virginia) Artillery
Hampden (Virginia) Artillery
Richmond Fayette Artillery
Blount's Virginia Battery

HOOD'S DIVISION

Maj. Gen. John B. Hood
Brig. Gen. Evander M. Law

LAW'S BRIGADE

Brig. Gen. Evander M. Law
Col. James L. Sheffield
4th Alabama
15th Alabama
44th Alabama
47th Alabama
48th Alabama

ROBERTSON'S BRIGADE

Brig. Gen. Jerome B. Robertson
3d Arkansas
1st Texas
4th Texas
5th Texas

ANDERSON'S BRIGADE

Brig. Gen. George T. Anderson

Lieut. Col. William Luffman
7th Georgia
8th Georgia
9th Georgia
11th Georgia
59th Georgia

BENNING'S BRIGADE
Brig. Gen. Henry L. Benning
2d Georgia
15th Georgia
17th Georgia
20th Georgia

ARTILLERY
Maj. Mathias W. Henry
Branch (North Carolina) Artillery
German (South Carolina) Artillery
Palmetto (South Carolina) Artillery
Rowan (North Carolina) Artillery

ARTILLERY RESERVE
Col. John B. Walton

ALEXANDER'S BATTALION
Col E. Porter Alexander
Ashland (Virginia) Artillery
Bedford (Virginia) Artillery
Brooks (South Carolina) Artillery
Madison (Louisiana) Artillery
Parker's Virginia Battery
Taylor's Virginia Battery

WASHINGTON ARTILLERY
Maj. Benjamin F. Eshleman
First Company
Second Company
Third Company
Fourth Company

EWELL'S CORPS
Lieut. Gen. Richard S. Ewell

EARLY'S DIVISION
Maj. Gen. Jubal A. Early

HAY'S BRIGADE
Brig. Gen. Harry T. Hays
5th Louisiana
6th Louisiana
7th Louisiana
8th Louisiana
9th Louisiana

SMITH'S BRIGADE
Brig. Gen. William Smith
31st Virginia
49th Virginia
52d Virginia

HOKE'S BRIGADE
Col. Isaac E. Avery
Col. Archibald C. Godwin
6th North Carolina
21st North Carolina
57th North Carolina

GORDON'S BRIGADE
Brig. Gen. John B. Gordon
13th Georgia
26th Georgia
31st Georgia
38th Georgia
60th Georgia
61st Georgia

ARTILLERY
Lieut. Col. Hilary P. Jones
Charlottesville (Virginia) Artillery
Courtney (Virginia) Artillery
Louisiana Guard Artillery
Staunton (Virginia) Artillery

JOHNSON'S DIVISION
Maj. Gen. Edward Johnson

STEUART'S BRIGADE
    Brig. Gen. George H. Steuart
    1st Maryland Battalion
    1st North Carolina
    3d North Carolina
    10th Virginia
    23d Virginia
    37th Virginia

STONEWALL BRIGADE
    Brig. Gen. James A. Walker
    2d Virginia
    4th Virginia
    5th Virginia
    27th Virginia
    33d Virginia

NICHOLLS'S BRIGADE
    Col. Jesse M. Williams
    1st Louisiana
    2d Louisiana
    10th Louisiana
    14th Louisiana
    15th Louisiana

JONES'S BRIGADE
    Brig. Gen. John M. Jones
    Lieut. Col. R. H. Dugan
    21st Virginia
    25th Virginia
    42d Virginia
    44th Virginia
    48th Virginia
    50th Virginia

ARTILLERY
    Maj. Joseph W. Latimer
    Capt. Charles I. Raine
    1st Maryland Battery
    Alleghany (Virginia) Artillery
    Chesapeake (Maryland) Artillery
    Lee (Virginia) Battery

RODES'S DIVISION
Maj. Gen. Robert E. Rodes

DANIEL'S BRIGADE
Brig. Gen. Junius Daniel
32d North Carolina
43d North Carolina
45th North Carolina
53d North Carolina
2d North Carolina Battalion

DOLES'S BRIGADE
Brig. Gen. George Doles
4th Georgia
12th Georgia
21st Georgia
44th Georgia

IVERSON'S BRIGADE
Brig. Gen. Alfred Iverson
5th North Carolina
12th North Carolina
20th North Carolina
23d North Carolina

RAMSEUR'S BRIGADE
Brig. Gen. Stephen D. Ramseur
2d North Carolina
4th North Carolina
14th North Carolina
30th North Carolina

O'NEAL'S BRIGADE
Col. Edward A. O'Neal
3d Alabama
5th Alabama
6th Alabama
12th Alabama
26th Alabama

ARTILLERY
Lieut. Col. Thomas H. Carter
Jeff. Davis (Alabama) Artillery
King William (Virginia) Artillery

Morris (Virginia) Artillery
Orange (Virginia) Artillery

ARTILLERY RESERVE
Col J. Thompson Brown

FIRST VIRGINIA ARTILLERY
Capt. Willis J. Dance
2d Richmond (Virginia) Howitzers
3d Richmond (Virginia) Howitzers
Powhatan (Virginia) Artillery
Rockbridge (Virginia) Artillery
Salem (Virginia) Artillery

NELSON'S BATTALION
Lieut. Col. William Nelson
Amherst (Virginia) Artillery
Fluvanna (Virginia) Artillery
Milledge's Georgia Battery

HILL'S CORPS
Lieut. Gen. Ambrose P. Hill

ANDERSON'S DIVISION
Maj. Gen. Richard H. Anderson

WILCOX'S BRIGADE
Brig. Gen. Cadmus M. Wilcox
8th Alabama
9th Alabama
10th Alabama
11th Alabama
14th Alabama

MAHONE'S BRIGADE
Brig. Gen. William Mahone
6th Virginia
12th Virginia
16th Virginia
41st Virginia
61st Virginia

WRIGHT'S BRIGADE
Brig. Gen. Ambrose R. Wright

    3d Georgia
    22d Georgia
    48th Georgia
    2d Georgia Battalion

PERRY'S BRIGADE
    Col. David Lang
    2d Florida
    5th Florida
    8th Florida

POSEY'S BRIGADE
    Brig. Gen. Carnot Posey
    12th Mississippi
    16th Mississippi
    19th Mississippi
    48th Mississippi

ARTILLERY (Sumter Battalion)
    Maj. John Lane
    Company A
    Company B
    Company C

HETH'S DIVISION
    Maj. Gen. Henry Heth
    Brig. Gen. J. Johnston Pettigrew

PETTIGREW'S BRIGADE
    Brig. Gen. J. Johnston Pettigrew
    Col. James K. Marshall
    11th North Carolina
    26th North Carolina
    47th North Carolina
    52d North Carolina

BROCKENBROUGH'S BRIGADE
    Col. John M. Brockenbrough
    40th Virginia
    47th Virginia
    55th Virginia
    22d Virginia Battalion

ARCHER'S BRIGADE
    Brig. Gen. James J. Archer

Col. Birkett D. Fry
Lieut. Col. Samuel G. Shepard
13th Alabama
5th Alabama Battalion
1st Tennessee
7th Tennessee
14th Tennessee

DAVIS'S BRIGADE
Brig. Gen. Joseph R. Davis
2d Mississippi
11th Mississippi
42d Mississippi
55th North Carolina

ARTILLERY
Lieut. Col. John J. Garnett
Donaldsonville (Louisiana) Artillery
Huger (Virginia) Artillery
Lewis (Virginia) Artillery
Norfolk Light Artillery Blues

PENDER'S DIVISION
Maj. Gen. William D. Pender
Brig. Gen. James H. Lane
Maj. Gen. Isaac R. Trimble
Brig. Gen. James H. Lane

PERRIN'S BRIGADE
Col. Abner Perrin
1st South Carolina
1st South Carolina Rifles
12th South Carolina
13th South Carolina
14th South Carolina

LANE'S BRIGADE
Brig. Gen. James H. Lane
Col. C. M. Avery
7th North Carolina
18th North Carolina
28th North Carolina

33d North Carolina
37th North Carolina

THOMAS'S BRIGADE
Brig. Gen. Edward L. Thomas
14th Georgia
35th Georgia
45th Georgia
49th Georgia

SCALES'S BRIGADE
Brig. Gen. Alfred M. Scales
Lieut. Col. George T. Gordon
Col. W. Lee J. Lowrance
13th North Carolina
16th North Carolina
22d North Carolina
34th North Carolina
38th North Carolina

ARTILLERY
Maj. William T. Poague
Albemarle (Virginia) Artillery
Charlotte (North Carolina) Artillery
Madison (Mississippi) Artillery
Brooke's Virginia Battery

ARTILLERY RESERVE
Col. R. Lindsay Walker

McINTOSH'S BATTALION
Maj. David G. McIntosh
Danville (Virginia) Artillery
Hardaway (Alabama) Artillery
2d Rockbridge (Virginia) Artillery
Johnson's Virginia Battery

PEAGRAM'S BATTALION
Maj. William J. Pegram
Capt. Ervin B. Brunson
Crenshaw's (Virginia) Battery
Fredericksburg (Virginia) Artillery
Letcher (Virginia) Battery

Pee Dee (South Carolina) Artillery
Purcell (Virginia) Artillery

CAVALRY

STUART'S DIVISION
Maj. Gen. J. E. B. Stuart

HAMPTON'S BRIGADE
Brig. Gen. Wade Hampton
Col. Laurence S. Baker
1st North Carolina
1st South Carolina
2d South Carolina
Cobb's (Georgia) Legion
Jeff. Davis Legion
Phillips (Georgia) Legion

JENKIN'S BRIGADE
Brig. Gen. Albert G. Jenkins
Col. Milton J. Ferguson
14th Virginia
16th Virginia
17th Virginia
34th Virginia Battalion
36th Virginia Battalion
Jackson's (Virginia) Battery

FITZ. LEE'S BRIGADE
Brig. Gen Fitzhugh Lee
1st Maryland Battalion
1st Virginia
2d Virginia
3d Virginia
4th Virginia
5th Virginia

W. H. F. LEE'S BRIGADE
Col. John R. Chambliss, Jr.
2d North Carolina
9th Virginia
10th Virginia
13th Virginia

JONES'S BRIGADE
>Brig. Gen William E. Jones
>6th Virginia
>7th Virginia
>11th Virginia

ROBERTSON'S BRIGADE
>Brig. Gen. Beverly Robertson
>4th North Carolina
>5th North Carolina

STUART'S HORSE ARTILLERY
>Maj. Robert F. Beckham
>Breathed's (Virginia) Battery
>Chew's (Virginia) Battery
>Griffin's (Maryland) Battery
>Hart's (South Carolina) Battery
>McGregor's (Virginia) Battery
>Moorman's (Virginia) Battery

IMBODEN'S COMMAND
>Brig. Gen. John D. Imboden
>18th Virginia Cavalry
>62d Virginia Infantry (Mounted)
>Virginia Partisan Rangers
>McClanahan's Virginia Battery

[*OR*, vol. 27, pt. 2, pp. 283–91]

NOTES

Introduction

1. U.S. War Department, *The War of Rebellion: A Compilation of the Official Records of the Union and Confederate Armies,* 70 volumes in 128 parts (Washington, DC: Government Printing Office, 1880–1901), series 1, vol. 16, pt. 1, 1088–94, and vol. 20, pt. 1, 184–85, 188–200, 663–72. (Hereinafter cited as *OR,* followed by appropriate volume, part, and page numbers; all series 1 unless noted.)

2. *OR,* vol. 9, 506–12, 530–35, 540–45, 551.

3. *OR,* vol. 11, pt. 2, 489–98. *OR,* vol. 12, pt. 2, 5–8, 176–79, 551–59. *OR,* vol. 19, pt. 1, 139–53. *OR,* vol. 19, pt. 2, 590–92, 593–94, 596, 600, 626–27.

4. *OR,* vol. 30, pt. 1, 47–62. *OR,* vol. 31, pt. 2, 92–97.

1. Before the Battle

1. Allan Nevins, *The War for the Union: War Becomes Revolution, 1862–1863* (New York: Charles Scribner's Sons, 1966), vol. 2, 298–301. James M. McPherson, *Battle Cry of Freedom* (New York: Oxford University Press, 1988), 590. Clifford Dowdey and Lewis H. Manarin, eds., *The Wartime Papers of Robert E. Lee* (Boston: Little Brown, 1961), 507–9.

2. Memorandum Book, entry for February 23, 1863, Jedediah Hotchkiss Papers, Library of Congress.

3. *OR*, vol. 27, pt. 2, 305. Edwin B. Coddington, *The Gettysburg Campaign: A Study in Command* (Dayton, OH: Morningside Bookshop, 1979), 8–9. Dowdey and Manarin, *The Wartime Papers of Robert E. Lee*, 505, 508, 531. A. L. Long, *Memoirs of Robert E. Lee* (New York: J. M. Stoddart, & Co., 1887; reprint, Secaucus, NJ: Blue and Grey Press, 1983), 269. "Letter from General A. L. Long," *Southern Historical Society Papers 4* (September 1887):120. Walter H. Taylor, "Second Paper by Colonel Walter H. Taylor," *Southern Historical Society Papers* 4 (September 1877): 124–25. Henry Heth, "Letter from Major General Heth," *Southern Historical Society Papers* 4 (October 1877): 152–53, 155. Walter H. Taylor, "The Campaign in Pennsylvania," in *The Annals of the War Written by Leading Participants North and South* (Philadelphia: Times Publishing Co., 1879; reprint, Dayton, OH: Morningside House, 1988), 305–6. Walter H. Taylor, *General Lee: His Campaigns in Virginia, 1861–1865* (Norfolk, VA: Husbaum Books, 1906; reprint, Lincoln: University of Nebraska Press, 1994), 180. Walter H. Taylor, *Four Years with General Lee* (Bloomington: Indiana University Press, 1962), 90–91. *OR*, vol. 27, pt. 2, 305. *OR*, vol. 27, pt. 3, 880–81, 930–31. James P. Smith, "General Lee at Gettysburg," *Southern Historical Society Papers* 33 (1905): 135–36. Frederick Maurice, ed., *An Aide de Camp of Robert E. Lee: Being the Papers of Charles Marshall* (Boston: Little, Brown, 1927; reprint, Whitefish, MT: Kessinger Publishing, 2005), 186–87, 188. Alan T. Nolen, "R. E. Lee and July 1 at Gettysburg," in Gary W. Gallagher, ed., *Lee the Soldier* (Lincoln, NE: University of Nebraska Press, 1996), 482–83. Glenn W. LaFantasie, *Twilight at Little Round Top* (Hoboken, NJ: John Wiley and Sons, 2005), 7. Richard Rollins, ed. *Pickett's Charge: Eyewitness Accounts* (Redondo Beach, CA: Rank and File Publications, 1994), xvii–xix.

4. *OR*, vol. 19, pt. 2, 590–91, 600, 604–05.

5. John B. Jones, *A Rebel War Clerk's Diary*, vol. 1 (Philadelphia: J. B. Lippincott and Company, 1866; reprint, Richmond, VA: Time-Life Books, 1983), 325. A. L. Long, *Memoirs of Robert E. Lee*, 269.

6. Dowdey and Manarin, eds., *The Wartime Papers of Robert E. Lee*, 438.

7. *OR*, vol. 27, pt. 3, 868–69.

8. *OR*, vol. 25, pt. 1, 789–94. *OR*, vol. 25, pt. 2, 810–11.

9. *OR*, vol. 25, pt. 2, 840. Douglas Southall Freeman, *Lee's Lieutenants: A Study in Command*. Vol. 2: *Cedar Mountain to Chancellorsville* (New York: Charles Scribner's Sons, 1943), 694–706.

10. *OR*, vol. 27, pt. 2, 283–90.

11. *OR*, vol. 27, pt. 2, 283–90. *OR*, vol. 25, pt. 2, 850–51. Jennings Cropper Wise, *The Long Arm of Lee*, 2 vol. (Richmond, VA: Owen's Publishing, 1988), 2:566–70.

12. *OR*, vol. 27, pt. 2, 290–91.

13. Edward G. Longacre, *The Man Behind the Guns: A Biography of Henry J. Hunt, Commander of Artillery, Army of the Potomac* (New York: A. S. Barnes and Company, 1977), 98–99. Ezra J. Warner, *Generals in Blue: Lives of the Union Commanders* (Baton Rouge, LA: Louisiana State University Press, 1964), 242.

14. *OR*, vol. 11, pt. 2, 238–39, 314–15. Matt Spruill III and Matt Spruill IV, *Echoes of Thunder: A Guide to the Seven Days Battles* (Knoxville: University of Tennessee Press, 2006), 215, 217, 221–25, 244, 251–56, 273.

15. *OR*, vol. 19, pt. 2, 188.

16. *OR*, vol. 19, pt. 1, 180. *OR*, vol. 21, 49.

17. *OR*, vol. 25, pt. 1, 157.

18. Longacre, *The Man Behind the Guns*, 150–51.

19. *OR*, vol. 25, pt. 2, 471–72. *OR*, vol. 27, pt. 1, 155–68. L. Van Loan Naisawald, *Grape and Canister: The Story of the Field Artillery of the Army of the Potomac, 1861–1865* (New York: Oxford University Press, 1960), 330–31.

20. Gregory A. Coco, *A Concise Guide to the Artillery at Gettysburg* (Gettysburg, PA: Thomas Publications, 1998), 70–75. *OR*, vol. 25, pt. 2, 471–72. *OR*, vol. 27, pt. 1, 155–68. Naisawald, *Grape and Canister*, 330–31.

21. *OR*, vol. 25, pt. 2, 471–72. *OR*, vol. 27, pt. 1, 155–68. Naisawald, *Grape and Canister*, 330–31.

22. *OR*, vol. 27, pt. 1, 231–32, 356–58, 748–49.

23. Ibid., 235, 584, 881–83.

24. Ibid., 238–40.

25. *Field Manual 17–95* (Washington, DC: U.S. Government Printing Office, 1996), Chapters 1, 3, and 4. Spruill and Spruill, *Echoes of Thunder,* 15, 17.

26. Ezra J. Warner, *Generals in Gray: Lives of the Confederate Commanders* (Baton Rouge, LA: Louisiana State University Press, 1959), 296–97.

27. Coddington, *The Gettysburg Campaign,* 77–80.

28. *OR,* vol. 27, pt. 3, 923.

29. *OR,* vol. 27, pt. 2, 692–93. Sears, *Gettysburg,* 106. Noah Andre Trudeau, *Gettysburg: A Testing of Courage* (New York: HarperCollins, 2002), 73–74.

30. *OR,* vol. 27, pt. 2, 297.

31. William Allen, "Memoranda of Conversations with General R. E. Lee, April 15, 1868," in Gallagher, *Lee the Soldier,* 13–14.

32. *OR,* vol. 27, pt. 2, 307. Maurice, *An Aide de Camp of Robert E. Lee,* 218.

33. G. Moxley Sorrel, *Recollections of a Confederate Staff Officer* (Wilmington, NC: Broadfoot Publishing, 1987), 154–55. James Longstreet, "Lee's Invasion of Pennsylvania," in Robert U. Johnson and Clarence C. Buel, eds., *Battles and Leaders of the Civil War,* 4 vols. (New York: Century Company, 1884–89), 3:249–51. *OR,* vol. 27, pt. 2, 318.

34. *OR,* vol. 27, pt. 2, 637.

35. Ernest B. Furgurson, *Chancellorsville, 1863* (New York: Alfred A. Knopf, 1992), 164–65. Stephen W. Sears. *Chancellorsville* (Boston: Houghton Mifflin, 1996), 257–59.

2. Wednesday, July 1, 1863

1. *OR,* vol. 27, pt. 2, 305–08, 358, 440, 442–43, 607. Coddington, *The Gettysburg Campaign,* 73–196.

2. Warner, *Generals in Blue,* 52–53.

3. *OR,* vol. 27, pt. 1, 914 and 926. Trudeau, *Gettysburg,* 141.

4. Trudeau, *Gettysburg,* 141.

5. *OR,* vol. 27, pt. 1, 926. *OR,* vol. 27, pt. 2, 607.

6. *OR,* vol. 27, pt. 1, 923–24.

7. *OR,* vol. 27, pt. 1, 144.

8. *Field Manual 100–5* (Washington, DC: U.S. Government Printing Office, 1986), 80, 142. *Field Manual 101–5–1* (Washington, DC: U.S. Government Printing Office, 1996), ch. 1.

9. *Field Manual 100–5,* 154–57. *Field Manual 100–5–1,* ch. 1. *OR,* vol. 27, pt. 1, 927.

10. *OR,* vol. 27, pt. 1, 927.

11. *OR,* vol. 27, pt. 3, 414–15, 416–17.

12. Warner, *Generals in Blue,* 396–97. Hal Bridges, *Lee's Maverick General* (Lincoln: University of Nebraska Press, 1991), 19. Freeman Cleaves, *The Rock of Chickamauga: The Life of General George H. Thomas* (Norman: University of Oklahoma Press, 1984), 25. *OR,* vol. 25, 157.

13. *OR,* vol. 27, pt. 3, 415–17.

14. *OR,* vol. 27, pt. 3, 416. *OR,* vol. 27, pt. 1, 114.

15. *OR,* vol. 27, pt. 1, 923–24.

16. *OR,* vol. 27, pt. 1, 244, 265, 701. Trudeau, *Gettysburg,* 169.

17. Sears, *Gettysburg,* 160. Trudeau, *Gettysburg,* 178. Harry W. Pfanz, *Gettysburg: The First Day* (Chapel Hill: University of North Carolina Press, 2001), 73–74. *OR,* vol. 27, pt. 1, 265. George Gordon Meade, *The Life and Letters of George Gordon Meade, Major-General United States Army,* 2 vols., ed. George Gordon Meade (New York: Charles Scribner's Sons, 1913), 2:35–36.

18. Abner Doubleday, *Chancellorsville and Gettysburg* (New York: Charles Scribner's Sons, 1886; reprint, Wilmington, NC: Broadfoot Publishing, 1989), 122.

19. *OR,* vol. 27, pt. 3, 414–15.

20. Trudeau, *Gettysburg,* 141. *OR,* vol. 27, pt. 1, 923–24. *OR,* vol. 27, pt. 3, 416.

21. *OR,* vol. 27, pt. 3, 458–59. Meade, *The Life and Letters,* 2:30.

22. *OR,* vol. 27, pt. 2, 316–17, 358, 443–44, 607.

23. Ibid., 607, 637.

24. Ibid., 317, 443–44.

25. Ibid., 467–68, 503–4, 552.

26. Ibid., 444, 468, 503–4, 552. Pfanz, *Gettysburg: The First Day*, 149–50, 227.

27. *OR*, vol. 27, pt. 2, 444.

28. Ibid., 444.

29. Warner, *Generals in Gray*, 263.

30. *OR*, vol. 27, pt. 2, 552–54

31. Ibid., 552–54.

32. Ibid., 444–45, 468.

33. Ibid., 317. Taylor, "Second Paper," 126–27.

34. Warner, *Generals in Gray*, 84–85. Jack D. Welsh, *Medical Histories of Confederate Generals* (Kent, OH: Kent State University Press, 1995), 64.

35. *OR*, vol. 27, pt. 2, 317–18.

36. Ibid., 445. Harry W. Pfanz, *Gettysburg: Culp's Hill and Cemetery Hill* (Chapel Hill: University of North Carolina Press, 1993), 77.

37. *OR*, vol. 27, pt. 2, 317–18, 445, 607. Pfanz, *Gettysburg: The First Day*, 342–44. *OR*, vol. 27, pt. 2, 503–4. Sun and moon data for July 1, 1863, Naval Oceanography Portal (Web site), http://aa.usno.navy.mil/data/docs/RS_OneDay.php. Smith, "General Lee at Gettysburg," 145–46.

38. *OR*, vol. 27, pt. 1, 357–58, 723–24, 748–49, 751. Gregory A. Coco, *A Concise Guide to the Artillery at Gettysburg* (Gettysburg, PA: Thomas Publications, 1998), 70, 72. Pfanz, *Gettysburg: The First Day*, 332–35. Pfanz, *Gettysburg: Culp's Hill and Cemetery Hill*, 57–59. Warren W. Hassler Jr., *Crisis at the Crossroads: The First Day at Gettysburg.* University: University of Alabama Press, 1970), 132–33. Herb S. Crumb, *The Eleventh Corps Artillery at Gettysburg* (Hamilton, NY: Edmonston Publishing, 1991), 13–15.

39. Spruill and Spruill, *Echoes of Thunder*, 244, 251, 264. Edwin C. Bearss, *The Union Artillery and Breckinridge's Attack* (Denver, CO: National Park Service Technical Information Center, 1959.) Matt Spruill and

Lee Spruill, *Winter Lightning: A Guide to the Battle of Stones River* (Knoxville: University of Tennessee Press, 2007), 200–209.

40. *OR*, vol. 27, pt. 2, 446.

41. Warner, *Generals in Blue*, 315–16.

42. *OR*, vol. 27, pt. 1, 61–62, 64, 66–67, 114, 144. *OR*, vol. 27, pt. 2, 307.

43. *OR*, vol. 27, pt. 1, 67, 68–69. *OR*, vol. 27, pt. 3, 375, 402, 415, 416–17, 419–20.

44. *OR*, vol. 27, pt. 2, 307, 358, 444, 607. *OR*, vol. 27, pt. 1, 144.

45. *OR*, vol. 27, pt. 1, 66–68.

46. *OR*, vol. 27, pt. 3, 418–19, 458–59. Meade, *The Life and Letters*, 2:29–30.

47. *OR*, vol. 27, pt. 3, 416, 458–59.

48. *OR*, vol. 27, pt. 1, 114–15, 366, 368, 924. *OR*, vol. 27, pt. 3, 461. Henry J. Hunt, "The Second Day at Gettysburg," in Johnson and Buel, *Battles and Leaders of the Civil War*, 3:291.

49. *OR*, vol. 27, pt. 1, 72.

3. Thursday, July 2, 1863

1. *OR*, vol. 27, pt. 2, 318, 358, 607–8. Boatner, *The Civil War Dictionary* (New York: David McKay Company, 1959), 819–20. Sun and moon data for July 1, 1863, Naval Oceanography Portal (Web site).

2. *OR*, vol. 27, pt. 1, 115–16, 144–45, 369, 482, 531, 592, 663, 758–59, 872.

3. *OR*, vol. 27, pt. 2, 318. James Longstreet, "Lee's Right Wing at Gettysburg," in Johnson and Buel, *Battles and Leaders of the Civil War*, 3:339 –40.

4. Warner, *Generals in Gray*, 192.

5. James Longstreet, "Lee's Invasion of Pennsylvania," in Johnson and Buel, *Battles and Leaders of the Civil War*, 3:246–47. Jeffry D. Wert, *General James Longstreet: The Confederacy's Most Controversial Soldier* (New York: Simon and Schuster, 1993), 206, 246–47, 266–67. Donald B. Sanger and Thomas R. Hay, *James Longstreet* (Baton Rouge: Louisiana State University Press, 1952), 117. *OR*, vol. 21, 1095–96.

6. Longstreet, "Lee's Right Wing at Gettysburg," 3:339–40. Harry W. Pfanz, *Gettysburg: The Second Day* (Chapel Hill: University of North Carolina Press, 1987), 26.

7. *Field Manual 3–0* (Washington, DC: Government Printing Office, 2001), ch. 7.

8. Ibid.

9. *OR,* vol. 27, pt. 2, 308, 318. Longstreet, "Lee's Right Wing at Gettysburg," 3:339–40.

10. Longstreet, "Lee's Right Wing at Gettysburg," 3:340. Pfanz, *Gettysburg: The Second Day,* 61, 105, 111–12.

11. *OR,* vol. 27, pt. 2, 318–19.

12. Pfanz, *Gettysburg: The Second Day,* 113. Boatner, *The Civil War Dictionary,* 819–20. Sanger and Hay, *James Longstreet,* 173–76. Sun and moon data for July 2, 1863, Naval Oceanography Portal (Web site).

13. Lafayette McLaws, "Gettysburg," *Southern Historical Society Papers* 7, no. 2 (1879): 69. Joseph B. Kershaw, "Kershaw's Brigade at Gettysburg," in Johnson and Buel, *Battles and Leaders of the Civil War,* 3:331.

14. McLaws, "Gettysburg," *SHSP* 7, 69. Kershaw, "Kershaw's Brigade at Gettysburg," 3:331–32.

15. McLaws, "Gettysburg," *SHSP* 7, 69. *OR,* vol. 27, pt. 2, 366–67.

16. Edward Porter Alexander, *Military Memoirs of a Confederate* (New York: Charles Scribner's Sons, 1907), 391–92. Edward Porter Alexander, *Fighting for the Confederacy,* edited by Gary W. Gallagher (Chapel Hill: University of North Carolina Press, 1989), 234–36.

17. McLaws, "Gettysburg," *SHSP* 7, 68–69.

18. *OR,* vol. 27, pt. 2, 367.

19. Coddington, *The Gettysburg Campaign,* 321, 335. Pfanz, *Gettysburg: The Second Day,* 86. *OR,* vol. 27, pt. 1, 159–61.

20. Pfanz, *Gettysburg: The Second Day,* 95–96. U.S. Congress, *Report of the Joint Committee on the Conduct of the War, Thirty-eighth Congress, General Sickles Testimony* (Washington, DC: U.S. Government Printing Office, 1865), 292. James A. Hessler, *Sickles at Gettysburg* (New York: Savas Beatie, 2009), 104, 116.

21. Warner, *Generals in Blue,* 446–47. *OR,* vol. 25, pt. 1, 405–6. Jay Luvaas and Harold Nelson, *The U.S. Army War College Guide to the Battles of Chancellorsville and Fredericksburg* (Carlisle, PA: South Mountain Press, 1988; reprint, Lawrence: University Press of Kansas, 1994), 248–55. Furgurson, *Chancellorsville, 1863,* 216–34. Sears, *Chancellorsville,* 312–13. Hessler, *Sickles at Gettysburg,* 60.

22. Hunt, "The Second Day at Gettysburg," 3:296–99. *OR,* vol. 27, pt. 1, 116, 581–82. W. A. Swanberg, *Sickles the Incredible* (New York: Charles Scribner's Sons, 1956), 206.

23. *OR,* vol. 27, pt. 1, 161–62, 592.

24. McLaws, "Gettysburg," *SHSP* 7, 69–70.

25. Kershaw, "Kershaw's Brigade at Gettysburg," 3:332. Evander M. Law, "The Struggle for Round Top," in Johnson and Buel, *Battles and Leaders of the Civil War,* 3:320.

26. Warner, *Generals in Gray,* 142–43.

27. Law, "The Struggle for Round Top," 3:321–22. Coddington, *The Gettysburg Campaign,* 382. Letter, Hood to Longstreet, *Southern Historical Society Papers* 4 (September 1877): 148–50.

28. *OR,* vol. 27, pt. 2, 318–19, 375, 428–29.

29. *OR,* vol. 27, pt. 1, 162–64, 592, 600, 634, 652, 663.

30. *OR,* vol. 27, pt. 2, 397, 404, 414. Law, "The Struggle for Round Top," 3:320.

31. *OR,* vol. 27, pt. 2, 391–96. Warner, *Generals in Gray,* 174–75.

32. *OR,* vol. 27, pt. 1, 234–35, 581–83. *OR,* vol. 27, pt. 2, 392–94, 405, 411.

33. *OR,* vol. 27, pt. 2, 414–15. Warner, *Generals in Gray,* 25–26.

34. Coddington, *The Gettysburg Campaign,* 342. Trudeau, *Gettysburg,* 255. *OR,* vol. 27, pt. 1, 266–67.

35. Coddington, *The Gettysburg Campaign,* 299 and 342. Trudeau, *Gettysburg,* 255 and 282. *OR,* vol. 27, pt. 1, 758–59, 778, and 825. Sears, *Gettysburg,* 246. Bradley M. Gottfried, *The Maps of Gettysburg* (New York and El Dorado Hills, California: Savas Beatie, 2007), 142. Pfanz, *Gettysburg: Culp's Hill and Cemetery Hill,* 111.

36. *OR*, vol. 27, pt. 1, 778 and 825–26. Gottfried, *The Maps of Gettysburg*, 227. Jesse H. Jones, "The Breastworks at Culp's Hill," in Johnson and Buel, *Battle and Leaders of the Civil War*, 3:316.

37. Warner, *Generals in Blue*, 186–87

38. Gottfried, *The Maps of Gettysburg*, 229. *OR*, vol. 27, pt. 1, 856–65.

39. *OR*, vol. 27, pt. 2, 470 and 504. Trudeau, *Gettysburg*, 291. Sears, *Gettysburg*, 230–31 and 256. Gottfried, *The Maps of Gettysburg*, 143. Pfanz, *Gettysburg: Culp's Hill and Cemetery Hill*, 79–80.

40. *OR*, vol. 27, pt. 2, 318–19 and 446. Pfanz, *Gettysburg: Culp's Hill and Cemetery Hill*, 205.

41. *OR*, vol. 27, pt. 2, 358, 429, 446, 504, and 543–44.

42. *OR*, vol. 27, pt. 1, 117, 759, and 773–74.

43. Pfanz, *Gettysburg: Culp's Hill and Cemetery Hill*, 194–95 and 200. Gottfried, *The Maps of Gettysburg*, 228–29. A. Wilson Greene, "'A Step All-Important and Essential to Victory': Henry W. Slocum and the Twelfth Corps," in Gary W. Gallagher, ed., *The Second Day at Gettysburg: Essays on Confederate and Union Leadership* (Kent, OH: Kent State Press, 1993), 114–17. Letter from Captain Charles P. Horton to John B. Bachelder, January 23, 1867, in *The Bachelder Papers*, 3 vols., ed. David L. Ladd and Audrey Ladd (Dayton, OH: Morningside House, 1994), 1:293–94. David W. Palmer, "King of the Hill," *America's Civil War Magazine*, July 2007, 51. R. L. Murray, *A Perfect Storm of Lead* (Walcott, NY: Benedum Books, 2000), 20. *OR*, vol. 27, pt. 1, 759 and 856. Milo M. Quaife, ed., *From the Cannon's Mouth: The Civil War Letters of General Alpheus S. Williams* (Lincoln: University of Nebraska Press, 1995), 229. George S. Greene, "The Breastworks at Culp's Hill," 3:317.

44. *OR*, vol. 27, pt. 1, 856–65. Murray, *A Perfect Storm of Lead*, 22–23. Pfanz, *Gettysburg: Culp's Hill and Cemetery Hill*, 211–13.

45. *OR*, vol. 27, pt. 2, 286 and 504. Pfanz, *Gettysburg: Culp's Hill and Cemetery Hill*, 207–10. Murray, *A Perfect Storm of Lead*, 25–38.

46. Gottfried, *The Maps of Gettysburg*, 240–49. Pfanz, *Gettysburg: Culp's Hill and Cemetery Hill*, 287.

4. Friday, July 3, 1863, and Afterward

1. *OR,* vol. 27, pt. 2, 446.

2. Trudeau, *Gettysburg,* 331, 373. *OR,* vol. 27, pt. 2, 446, 504, 543–44.

3. *OR,* vol. 27, pt. 2, 447. *OR,* vol. 27, pt. 1, 261, 266–67, 759, 773, 856. Alpheus S. Williams, *From the Cannon's Mouth* (Detroit, MI: Wayne State University Press, 1959; reprint, Lincoln: University of Nebraska Press, 1995), 227.

4. *OR,* vol. 27, pt. 1, 759, 773–74, 856. Williams, *From the Cannon's Mouth,* 227–29.

5. *OR,* vol. 27, pt. 1, 759, 856–57. *OR,* vol. 27, pt. 2, 504, 509–10.

6. *OR,* vol. 27, pt. 2, 320.

7. Warner, *Generals in Blue,* 559–60.

8. Ibid., 451–52.

9. *OR,* vol. 27, pt. 1, 759–61, 774–75, 780, 827.

10. *OR,* vol. 27, pt. 1, 761, 774–75, 780–81, 870, 896, 899. *OR,* vol. 27, pt. 2, 447–48, 504–5, 511. Murray, *A Perfect Storm of Lead,* 42–49. Gottfried, *The Maps of Gettysburg,* 240–49.

11. *OR,* vol. 27, pt. 2, 320, 447. Carol Reardon, *Pickett's Charge in History and Memory,* (Chapel Hill: University of North Carolina Press, 1997), 5. Henry B. McClellan, *I Rode with Jeb Stuart* (New York: DaCapo Press, 1994), 337.

12. *OR,* vol. 27, pt. 2, 320. James Longstreet, *From Manassas to Appomattox* (Secaucus, NJ: Blue and Grey Press), 386. Longstreet, *"Lee's Right Wing at Gettysburg,"* 3:342. Maurice, *An Aide de Camp of Robert E. Lee,* 238–39. Trudeau, *Gettysburg,* 436. Sears, *Gettysburg,* 357–58.

13. *OR,* vol. 27, pt. 2, 318. Reardon, *Pickett's Charge in History,* 5. Rollins, *Pickett's Charge,* xix.

14. Kent Masterson Brown, *Retreat from Gettysburg* (Chapel Hill, N.C: University of North Carolina Press, 2005), 387–89.

15. *OR,* vol. 27, pt. 2, 318–20, 447, 504.

16. *OR,* vol. 27, pt. 2, 320, 363–64, 444–45, 447, 607–8.

17. *OR,* vol. 27, pt. 2, 320, 351–52, 359, 608, 614–15, 632. Gottfried, *The Maps of Gettysburg,* 250–51.

18. *OR,* vol. 27, pt. 2, 623–24. OR, vol. 27, pt. 1, 261–62.

19. Edwin C. Fishel, *The Secret War for the Union* (Boston: Houghton Mifflin, 1996), 528 and 530. Coddingtin, *Gettysburg,* 248.

20. John Gibbon, *Personal Recollections of the Civil War* (New York: G. P. Putnam's Sons, 1928. Reprint, Dayton, OH: Morningside House, 1988), 145. Meade, *The Life and Letters,* 2:97. *OR,* vol. 51, pt. 1, 1068. *OR,* vol. 27, pt. 1, 663. Henry J. Hunt, "The Third Day at Gettysburg," in Johnson and Buel, *Battles and Leaders of the Civil War,* 3:371–72.

21. *OR,* vol. 27, pt. 2, 448. Longstreet, "Lee's Right Wing at Gettysburg," 3:349. Law, "The Struggle for Round Top," 3:330.

22. *OR,* vol. 27, pt. 2, 309, 322, 346 (20,451 casualties). Sears, *Gettysburg,* 498 (22,625 casualties), 532–43. Coddington, *The Gettysburg Campaign,* 536 (20,451 casualties). Trudeau, *Gettysburg,* 529 (22,874 casualties). Robert Krick, *The Gettysburg Death Roster: The Confederate Dead at Gettysburg* (Dayton, OH: Press of Morningside Bookshop, 1993), 17 (22,198 casualties). Other sources give Lee's casualties as 28,000. This is total campaign casualties, not just July 1–3. Alexander, *Military Memoirs of a Confederate,* 434.

23. *OR,* vol. 27, pt. 2, 309. Sears, *Gettysburg,* 472.

24. *OR,* vol. 27, pt. 2, 309.

25. Coddington, *Gettysburg,* 535–37.

26. *OR,* vol. 27, pt. 1, 74–75 and 78. Meade, *The Life and Letters,* 2:111–12. Trudeau, *Gettysburg,* 534.

27. Sears, *Gettysburg,* 516–31. OR, vol. 27, pt. 1, 78 and 173–87. *OR,* vol. 27, pt. 3, 520.

Conclusion

1. *OR,* vol. 27, pt. 2, 311. .

2. *OR,* vol. 27, pt. 2, 322. Brown, *Retreat from Gettysburg,* 93, 118. Sears, *Gettysburg,* 472.

3. John D. Imboden, "The Confederate Retreat from Gettysburg," in Johnson and Buel, *Battles and Leaders of the Civil War,* 3:422–24. OR,

vol. 27, pt. 1, 198. Sears, *Gettysburg*, 498. Coddington, *The Gettysburg Campaign*, 537. Brown, *Retreat from Gettysburg*, 384.

4. *OR*, vol. 27, pt. 2, 309, 322–23, 361, 448, 608. Brown, *Retreat from Gettysburg*, 178. Glenn Tucker, *High Tide at Gettysburg: The Campaign in Pennsylvania* (Indianapolis: Bobbs-Merrill, 1958; reprint, New York: Konecky & Konecky, 1994), 386–87.

5. *OR*, vol. 27, pt. 1, 117–18, 145–47, 222–23, 663–64. *OR*, vol. 27, pt. 2, 323. Meade, *The Life and Letters*, 2:119–31. Brown, *Retreat from Gettysburg*, 188.

6. *OR*, vol. 27, pt. 2, 324. *OR*, vol. 27, pt. 1, 118.

7. *OR*, vol. 21, 142, 562. *OR*, vol. 25, pt. 1, 192, 809. Maurice, *An Aide de Camp of Robert E. Lee*, 188. Steven E. Woodworth, *Davis and Lee at War* (Lawrence: University Press of Kansas, 1995), 214–15.

8. *OR*, vol. 25, pt. 2, 725. *OR*, series 4, vol. 2, 192–93, 351. Taylor, *General Lee*, 162. Long, *Memoirs of Robert E. Lee*, 247. Dowdey and Manarin, *The Wartime Papers of Robert E. Lee*, 435, 638. Brown, *Retreat from Gettysburg*, 388.

9. Sears, *Gettysburg*, 57, 498. Coddington, *The Gettysburg Campaign*, 249. Andrew A. Humphreys, *The Virginia Campaign of '64 and '65* (New York: Charles Scribner's Sons, 1883; reprint, Wilmington, NC: Broadfoot Publishing, 1989), 17. Douglas Southall Freeman, ed., *Lee's Dispatches: Unpublished Letters of General Robert E. Lee to Jefferson Davis and the War Department of the Confederate States of America, 1862–65* (New York: G. P. Putnam's Sons, 1915; reprint, Baton Rouge: Louisiana State University Press, 1994), 122–24.

BIBLIOGRAPHY

Alexander, Edward Porter. *Fighting for the Confederacy.* Edited by Gary W. Gallagher. Chapel Hill: University of North Carolina Press, 1989.

————. *Military Memoirs of a Confederate.* New York: Charles Scribner's Sons, 1907.

Bearss, Edwin C. *The Union Artillery and Breckinridge's Attack.* Denver, CO: National Park Service Technical Information Center, 1959.

Boatner, Mark W. *The Civil War Dictionary.* New York: David McKay Company, 1959.

Bridges, Hal. *Lee's Maverick General: Daniel Harvey Hill.* Lincoln: University of Nebraska Press, 1991.

Brown, Kent Masterson. *Retreat from Gettysburg: Lee Logistics and the Pennsylvania Campaign.* Chapel Hill: University of North Carolina Press, 2005.

Cleaves, Freeman. *The Rock of Chickamauga: The Life of General George H. Thomas.* Norman: University of Oklahoma Press, 1984.

Coco, Gregory A. *A Concise Guide to the Artillery at Gettysburg.* Gettysburg, PA: Thomas Publications, 1998.

Coddington, Edwin B. *The Gettysburg Campaign: A Study in Command.* Dayton, OH: Press of Morningside Bookshop, 1979.

Crumb, Herb S. *The Eleventh Corps Artillery at Gettysburg.* Hamilton, NY: Edmonston Publishing, 1991.

Doubleday, Abner. *Chancellorsville and Gettysburg.* New York: Charles Scribner's Sons, 1886; reprint, Wilmington, NC: Broadfoot Publishing, 1989.

Dowdey, Clifford, and Manarin, Louis H., eds. *The Wartime Papers of Robert E. Lee.* Boston, MA: Little, Brown, 1961.

Field Manual 3–0. Washington, DC: U.S. Government Printing Office, 2001

Field Manual 17–95. Washington, DC: U.S. Government Printing Office, 1996.

Field Manual 100–5. Washington, DC: U.S. Government Printing Office, 1986.

Field Manual 101–5–1. Washington, DC: U.S. Government Printing Office, 1996.

Fishel, Edwin C. *The Secret War for the Union.* Boston: Houghton Mifflin, 1996.

Freeman, Douglas Southall. *Lee's Lieutenants: A Study in Command.* Vol. 2: *Cedar Mountain to Chancellorsville.* New York: Charles Scribner's Sons, 1943.

———, ed. *Lee's Dispatches: Unpublished Letters of General Robert E. Lee to Jefferson Davis and the War Department of the Confederate States of America, 1862–65.* New York: G. P. Putnam's Sons, 1915; reprint, Baton Rouge: Louisiana State University Press, 1994.

Furgurson, Ernest B. *Chancellorsville, 1863: The Souls of the Brave.* New York: Alfred A. Knopf, 1992.

Gallagher, Gary W., ed. *Lee the Soldier.* Lincoln: University of Nebraska Press, 1996.

———. *The Second Day at Gettysburg: Essays on Confederate and Union Leadership.* Kent, OH: Kent State University Press, 1993.

Gibbon, John. *Personal Recollections of the Civil War.* New York: G. P. Putnam's Sons, 1928; reprint, Dayton, OH: Morningside House, 1988.

Gottfried, Bradley M. *The Maps of Gettysburg.* New York and El Dorado Hills, California: Savas Beatie, 2007.

Greene, A. Wilson. "'A Step All-Important and Essential to Victory': Henry W. Slocum and the Twelfth Corps." In *Second Day at Gettysburg: Essays on Confederate and Union Leadership.* Edited by Gary Gallagher, 87–135. Kent, OH: Kent State Press, 1993.

Greene, George S. "The Breastworks at Culp's Hill." In *Battle and Leaders of the Civil War.* 4 vols. Edited by Robert U. Johnson and Clarence C. Buel. New York: Century Company, 1884–89.

Harman, Troy D. *Lee's Real Plan at Gettysburg.* Mechanicsburg, PA: Stackpole Books, 2003.

Hassler, Warren W., Jr. *Crisis at the Crossroads: The First Day at Gettysburg.* University: University of Alabama Press, 1970.

Hessler, James A. *Sickles at Gettysburg.* New York and El Dorado Hill, CA: Savas Beatie, 2009.

Heth, Henry. "Letter from General Heth." *Southern Historical Society Papers* 4 (June 1877): 151–60.

Hood, John B. "Letter from General Hood." *Southern Historical Society Papers* 4 (June 1877): 145–50.

Hotchkiss, Jedediah. Memorandum Book. Jedediah Hotchkiss Papers, Library of Congress.

Humphreys, Andrew A. *The Virginia Campaign of '64 and '65.* New York: Charles Scribner's Sons, 1883; reprint, Wilmington, NC: Broadfoot Publishing, 1989.

Hunt, Henry J. "The Second Day at Gettysburg." In *Battles and Leaders of the Civil War.* Vol. 3. Edited by Robert U. Johnson and Clarence C. Buel, 290–313. New York: Century Company, 1884–89.

———. "The Third Day at Gettysburg." In *Battles and Leaders of the Civil War.* Vol. 3. Edited by Robert U. Johnson and Clarence C. Buel, 369–85. New York: Century Company, 1884–89.

Imboden, John D. "The Confederate Retreat from Gettysburg." In *Battles and Leaders of the Civil War.* Vol. 3. Edited by Robert U. Johnson and Clarence C. Buel, 420–29. New York: Century Company, 1884–89.

Jones, Jesse H. "The Breastworks at Culp's Hill." In *Battles and Leaders of the Civil War.* Vol. 3. Edited by Robert U. Johnson and Clarence C. Buel, 316. New York: Century Company, 1884–89.

Jones, John B. *A Rebel War Clerk's Diary*. 2 vols. Philadelphia, PA: J. B. Lippincott, 1866; reprint, Richmond, VA: Time-Life Books, 1983.

Kershaw, Joseph B. "Kershaw's Brigade at Gettysburg." In *Battles and Leaders of the Civil War*. Vol. 3. Edited by Robert U. Johnson and Clarence C. Buel, 331–38. New York: Century Company, 1884–89.

Krick, Robert. *The Gettysburg Death Roster: The Confederate Dead at Gettysburg*. Dayton, OH: Morningside Bookshop, 1993.

Ladd, David L., and Audrey J. Ladd, eds. *The Bachelder Papers*. 3 vols. Dayton, OH: Morningside House, 1994.

LaFantasie, Glenn W. *Twilight at Little Round Top*. Hoboken, NJ: John Wiley and Sons, 2005.

Law, Evander M. "The Struggle for 'Round Top.'" In *Battles and Leaders of the Civil War*. Vol. 3. Edited by Robert U. Johnson and Clarence C. Buel, 318–30. New York: Century Company, 1884–89.

Long, A. L. "Letter from General A. L. Long." *Southern Historical Society Papers* 4 (September 1877): 66–69.

———. *Memoirs of Robert E. Lee*. Secaucus, NJ: Blue and Grey Press, 1983.

Longacre, Edward G. *The Man Behind the Guns: A Biography of Henry J. Hunt, Commander of Artillery, Army of the Potomac*. New York: A. S. Barnes and Company, 1977.

Longstreet, James. *From Manassas to Appomattox*. Secaucus, NJ: Blue and Grey Press, 1984.

———. "Lee's Invasion of Pennsylvania." In *Battles and Leaders of the Civil War*. Vol. 3. Edited by Robert U. Johnson and Clarence C. Buel, 244–51. New York: Century Company, 1884–89.

———. "Lee's Right Wing at Gettysburg." In *Battles and Leaders of the Civil War*. Vol. 3. Edited by Robert U. Johnson and Clarence C. Buel, 339–54. New York: Century Company, 1884–89.

Luvaas, Jay, and Harold Nelson. *The U.S. Army War College Guide to the Battles of Chancellorsville and Fredericksburg*. Carlisle, PA: South Mountain Press, 1988; reprint, Lawrence: University Press of Kansas, 1994.

Maurice, Frederick, ed. *An Aide de Camp of Robert E. Lee: Being the Papers of Charles Marshall*. Boston: Little, Brown, 1927; reprint, Whitefish, MT: Kessinger Publishing, 2005.

McClellan, Henry B. *I Rode with Jeb Stuart.* New York: DaCapo Press, 1994.

McLaws, Lafayette. "Gettysburg." *Southern Historical Society Papers* 7, no. 2 (1879): 64–90.

McPherson, James M. *Battle Cry of Freedom.* New York: Oxford University Press, 1988.

Meade, George Gordon. *The Life and Letters of George Gordon Meade, Major-General United States Army,* 2 vols. Edited by George Gordon Meade. New York: Charles Scribner's Sons, 1913.

Murray, R. L. *A Perfect Storm of Lead.* Walcott, New York: Benedum Books, 2000.

Naisawald, L. Van Loan. *Grape and Canister: The Story of the Field Artillery of the Army of the Potomac, 1861–1865.* New York: Oxford University Press, 1960.

Nevins, Allan. *The War for the Union: War Becomes Revolution, 1862–1863.* Vol. 2. New York: Charles Scribner's Sons, 1960.

Nolen, Alan T. "R. E. Lee and July 1 at Gettysburg." In Gary W. Gallagher, ed., *Lee: The Soldier* (Lincoln: University of Nebraska Press, 1996), 482–83.

Palmer, David W. "King of the Hill." *America's Civil War Magazine,* July 2007, 51.

Pfanz, Harry W. *Gettysburg: Culp's Hill and Cemetery Hill.* Chapel Hill: University of North Carolina Press, 1993.

———. *Gettysburg: The Second Day.* Chapel Hill: University of North Carolina Press, 1987.

———. *Gettysburg: The First Day.* Chapel Hill: University of North Carolina Press, 2001.

Quaife, Milo M., ed. *From the Cannon's Mouth: The Civil War Letters of General Alpheus S. Williams.* Lincoln: University of Nebraska Press, 1995.

Reardon, Carol. *Pickett's Charge in History and Memory.* Chapel Hill: University of North Carolina Press, 1997.

Rollins, Richard, ed. *Pickett's Charge: Eyewitness Accounts.* Redondo Beach, CA: Rank and File Publications, 1994.

Sanger, Donald B., and Thomas R. Hay. *James Longstreet.* Baton Rogue: Louisiana State University Press, 1952.

Sears, Stephen W. *Chancellorsville.* Boston: Houghton Mifflin, 1996.

———. *Gettysburg.* Boston: Houghton Mifflin, 2003.

Smith, James P. "General Lee at Gettysburg." *Southern Historical Society Papers* 33 (1905): 135–36.

Sorrel, G. Moxley. *Recollections of a Confederate Staff Officer.* Wilmington, NC: Broadfoot Publishing , 1987.

Spruill, Matt, III, and Matt Spruill IV. *Echoes of Thunder: A Guide to the Seven Days Battles.* Knoxville: University of Tennessee Press, 2006.

Spruill, Matt, and Lee Spruill. *Winter Lightning: A Guide to the Battle of Stones River.* Knoxville: University of Tennessee Press, 2007.

Swanberg, W. A. *Sickles the Incredible.* New York: Charles Scribner's Sons, 1956.

Taylor, Walter H. "The Campaign in Pennsylvania." In *The Annals of the War Written by Leading Participants North and South,* 305–18. Philadelphia: Times Publishing Co., 1879; reprint, Dayton, OH: Morningside Bookshop, 1988.

———. *Four Years with General Lee.* Bloomington: Indiana University Press, 1962.

———. *General Lee: His Campaigns in Virginia, 1861–1865.* Norfolk, VA: Nussbaum Books, 1906; reprint, Lincoln: University of Nebraska Press, 1994.

———. "Second Paper by Colonel Walter H. Taylor." *Southern Historical Society Papers* 4 (September 1877): 124–39.

Trudeau, Noah Andre. *Gettysburg: A Testing of Courage.* New York: HarperCollins, 2002.

Tucker, Glenn. *High Tide at Gettysburg: The Campaign in Pennsylvania.* Indianapolis: Bobbs-Merrill, 1958; reprint, New York: Konecky & Konecky, 1994.

U.S. Congress. *Report of the Joint Committee on the Conduct of the War, Thirty-eighth Congress, General Sickles Testimony.* Washington, DC: U.S. Government Printing Office, 1865.

U.S. War Department. *The War of Rebellion: A Compilation of the Official Records of the Union and Confederate Armies*. 70 volumes in 128 parts. Washington, DC: U.S. Government Printing Office, 1880–1901.

Warner, Ezra J. *Generals in Blue: Lives of the Union Commanders*. Baton Rouge: Louisiana State University Press, 1964.

——. *Generals in Gray: Lives of the Confederate Commanders*. Baton Rouge: Louisiana State University Press, 1959.

Welsh, Jack D. *Medical Histories of Confederate Generals*. Kent, OH: Kent State University Press, 1995.

Wert, Jeffry D. *General James Longstreet: The Confederacy's Most Controversial Soldier*. New York: Simon and Schuster, 1993.

Williams, Alpheus S. *From the Cannon's Mouth*. Detroit, MI: Wayne State University Press, 1959; reprint, Lincoln: University of Nebraska Press, 1995.

Wise, Jennings Cropper. *The Long Arm of Lee*. 2 vols. Richmond, VA: Owens Publishing, 1988.

Woodworth, Steven E. *Davis and Lee at War*. Lawrence: University Press of Kansas, 1995.

INDEX

Decisions at Gettysburg was designed and typeset on a Macintosh OS 10.5 computer system using InDesign software. The body text is set in 10/13 Adobe Caslon Pro and display type is set in Adobe Caslon Pro. This book was designed and typeset by Stephanie Thompson and manufactured by Thomson-Shore, Inc.